口未来

hared Future

北京 2022 年冬奥会和冬残奥会遗产报告（赛后）

Olympic and Paralympic Winter Games
Beijing 2022 Legacy Report(post-Games)

北京 2022 年冬奥会和冬残奥会组织委员会
北京体育大学 著

生活·读书·新知 三联书店

图书在版编目（CIP）数据

北京 2022 年冬奥会和冬残奥会遗产报告.赛后／北京 2022 年冬奥会和冬残奥会组织委员会，
北京体育大学著.—北京：生活·读书·新知三联书店，2024.2
ISBN 978－7－108－07728－8

Ⅰ.北… Ⅱ.①中… ②北… Ⅲ.①冬季奥运会研究报告－北京－2022 ②世界残疾人运动会－
奥运会－研究报告－北京－2022
Ⅳ.① G811.212 ② G811.228

中国版本图书馆 CIP 数据核字（2023）第 195024 号

责任编辑　王婧娅
装帧设计　崔欣晔　李　思
责任印制　洪江龙
出版发行　生活·讀書·新知 三联书店
　　　　　（北京市东城区美术馆东街 22 号）
邮　　编　100010
印　　刷　上海雅昌艺术印刷有限公司
版　　次　2024 年 2 月 4 日第 1 版
　　　　　2024 年 2 月 4 日第 1 次印刷
开　　本　710 毫米 × 1000 毫米　1/16　印张 15.75
字　　数　197 千字　图 86 幅
定　　价　188.00 元

北京冬奥组委总体策划部

李　森　王仁华　刘兴华　刘　楠　祁　轩
姜　巍　樊佩杰　黄　颖　辛宇晨

北京体育大学

曹卫东　高　峰　白宇飞　邹新娴　蒋依依
杨建荣　洪建平　时　婧　刘润芝　宋赫民
谢　婷　张佑印　马天平　杨占东　陈　希
吴　迪　于　环　范松梅　史书菡　方　琰
罗士洄　左　文　刘文静　洪鹏飞　何道刚

序 言

北京 2022 年冬奥会和冬残奥会（以下简称"北京冬奥会"）是中国重要历史节点的重大标志性活动，在中国政府的坚强领导下，在与国际奥委会、国际残奥会和国际冬季单项体育组织紧密合作下，全面贯彻落实"绿色、共享、开放、廉洁"办奥理念，经历 7 年的艰辛筹办，克服各种困难挑战，中国人民与世界人民一道如期向世界奉献了一届"简约、安全、精彩"的奥运盛会，取得了圆满成功，实现了对国际社会的庄严承诺，赢得了全世界高度赞誉，北京成为全球首个"双奥之城"，再一次书写了奥林匹克运动历史，再一次共享奥林匹克荣光。

北京冬奥会不仅是一场精彩纷呈的体育盛会，更创造和带来了丰厚的冬奥遗产。"三亿人参与冰雪运动"的宏伟目标如期实现，极大地带动了全国大众和青少年参与冰雪运动的热情，开启了全球冰雪运动的新时代。冬奥筹办有力带动京张地区和主办城市高质量发展，带动区域交通设施相连通、生态环境联防联控、产业发展互补互促、公共服务共建共享，首钢成为城市复兴新地标，延庆建设最美冬奥城，张家口打造国际冰雪旅游度假目的地，交出了冬奥筹办和带动本地发展两份优异答卷。广大民众也从冬奥筹办中得到了真正的实惠，冰雪产业助力脱贫攻坚，就业机会大幅增加，生活条件日益改善，无障碍环境显著提升，残疾人事业快速发展，志愿服务精神广泛弘扬，全社会文明程度进一步提升。这些丰硕的遗产成果已经在北京冬奥组委发布的系列赛前遗产报告中详细阐述。

本报告为赛后遗产报告，主要介绍传承和利用冬奥遗产成果，持续推广普及冰雪运动，带动城市和区域高质量发展，促进社会文明进步的发展思路、规划和主要措施，分为冰雪运动普及发展、场馆赛后利用、冰雪产业发展、主办城市发展、京张体育文化旅游带建设、传承奥运文化和各项社会事业发展等 7 个篇章。

目 录

第六章

深入开展奥林匹克教育，持续推动社会文明进步

第七章

传承利用冬奥文化遗产，为美好未来注入生机活力

第一章

持续推动冰雪运动普及及发展
带动全民健身事业走向纵深

北京冬奥会的筹办和举办极大带动了中国冰雪运动的跨越式发展，全国冰雪运动参与人数达到3.46亿人，"带动三亿人参与冰雪运动"已从愿景变为现实。这也是北京冬奥会带给全球冬季运动和奥林匹克运动最为重要的遗产，它显著壮大了全球冰雪运动参与人群，重塑了世界冰雪运动的版图，为全球冰雪运动、冰雪产业的蓬勃发展提供了广阔空间。北京冬奥会的成功举办不是终点，普及发展冰雪运动、带动全民健身事业高质量发展是中国的一项长期国策，是推动体育强国、健康中国建设的有力途径。未来，中国将持续为冰雪运动普及发展提供长期政策保障，持续推动大众冰雪运动蓬勃发展，建设更多优质冰雪场地设施，健全冬季运动后备人才培养体系，不断提升冰雪运动竞技水平。

● 北京冬奥会后，位于国家游泳中心（水立方/冰立方）南广场地下的冰上运动中心对公众开放

一、持续推动大众冰雪运动蓬勃发展

北京冬奥会点燃了广大民众参与冰雪运动的热情，冰雪运动在大江南北、长城内外呈现出前所未有的发展活力和态势。但是，对比中国人口基数和不断提升的消费能力，中国的冰雪运动还有很大的发展潜力。未来，中国将持续为冰雪运动普及发展提供良好的政策环境，广泛推广冰雪文化，持续举办好各类群众性品牌冰雪活动，扩大冰雪运动在广大青少年中的参与率和覆盖面，巩固和拓展"带动三亿人参与冰雪运动"成果。

加大冰雪运动宣传推广力度。普及冬季运动知识，拍摄和制作各类冰雪运动宣传片、动画、视频、歌曲，编发冬季运动普及读本、知识手册、健身指导及运动防护手册，引导广大群众关注、喜爱、参与冰雪运动。拓宽冰雪文化传播渠道，搭建信息传播平台，鼓励电视、广播、报纸、杂志等媒体开办冰雪运动节目和专栏，广泛组织开展线上冰雪活动，加强对冰雪文化、冰雪知识和赛事活动的宣传。

3.46 亿

全国冰雪运动参与人数

最重要

北京冬奥会遗产

重塑

世界冰雪运动版图

第8届北京市民快乐冰雪季

　　北京市民快乐冰雪季创办于2014年，由北京市政府主办，迄今已连续举办8届。其中第8届冰雪季于2021年12月—2022年4月举办，通过组织开展线上线下同步的各类活动，吸引全市各区群众参与。活动期间，通过答题抢票等方式向市民免费发放累计12万张冰雪公益体验券，带动更多群众走上冰场雪场。冰雪季全市26家公园共开设34处场地，推出了丰富多样的冰雪活动，共有140万人次参与。此外，由北京人民广播电台在"1025动生活"和"体育的101种可能"两档节目中开设空中大讲堂，普及冬奥会知识和冰雪运动常识，带动更多市民了解冰雪运动。大讲堂共开设198期，受众超5940万人次。据统计，第8届冰雪季共举办冰雪活动达9075场，创1690万人次参与的新高（不含空中大讲堂）。随着冰雪季系列活动品牌影响力的不断扩大，未来其将在助力北京群众冰雪运动高质量发展中持续发挥重要作用。

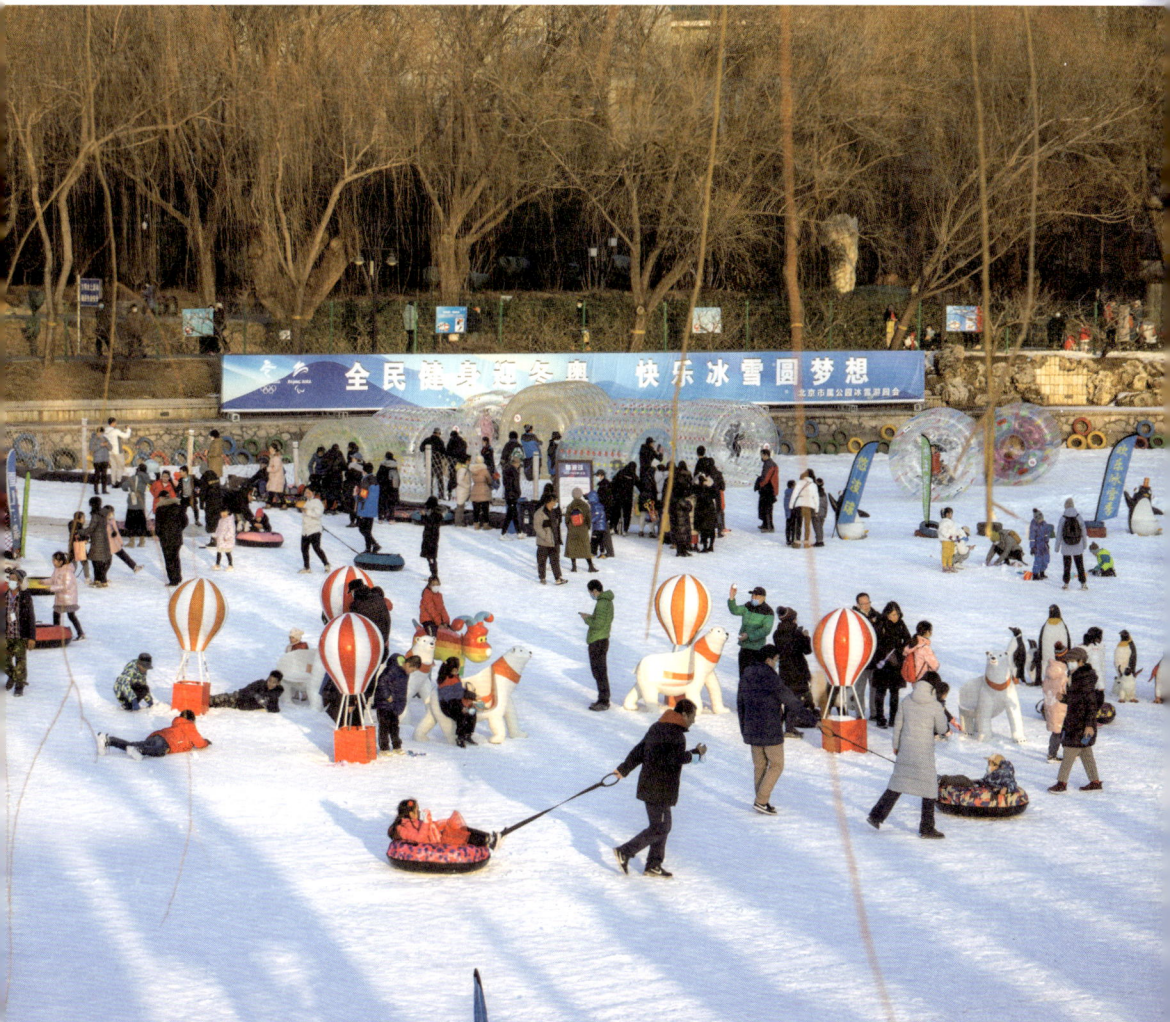

● 第8届北京市民快乐冰雪季期间紫竹院公园举办"冰雪游园会"

持续举办群众性冰雪活动。继续发挥"全国大众冰雪季"等群众性品牌冰雪活动的引领、示范、带动作用，持续扩大活动的受众人群和城市覆盖范围，吸引更多群众感受和体验冰雪运动乐趣。同时，继续开展"全国大众欢乐冰雪周"等非雪季群众性冰雪活动，拓展冰雪运动时间跨度，突破季节限制。全国各地依托当地自然和人文资源，因地制宜，持续创新发展形式多样、特色鲜明、群众喜闻乐见的品牌冰雪赛事活动。针对残疾人群体，将继续举办"中国残疾人冰雪运动季"，创办适合残疾人参与的冰雪项目和赛事，推广冬残奥项目，传播冬残奥理念，为残疾人参与冰雪运动创造更好的条件。

完善群众冰雪运动规范标准。加强冰雪运动基础性工作，加快研究制定一批冰雪运动规范化发展急需的技术标准和规范。研究制定冰雪运动大众等级标准和实施办法，推进统一规范的评定工作，促进群众性冰雪运动技能水平不断提高。完善群众性冰雪运动赛事标准，研究制定大众冰雪赛事标准与服务指南，用规范专业的赛事标准和技术服务指导大众冰雪赛事，大力推动办赛由经验化向标准化、规范化转变。

扩大青少年冰雪运动普及推广。深入实施校园冰雪计划，继续推进"奥林匹克教育示范校"和"冰雪运动特色学校"建设，扩大示范效应。支持南方地区有条件的中小学持续开展仿冰、仿雪课程，推动青少年"轮（滑）转（滑）冰"计划。鼓励有条件的学校建立常态化校园冬季运动竞赛机制，举办冬季运动会或冬季运动节，推动形成以学生社团为主体的青少年冰雪运动发展格局。持续举办世界雪日暨国际儿童滑雪节、青少年冰雪冬夏令营、青少年公益冰雪系列等活动，培养青少年儿童冰雪运动兴趣和爱好。加强青少年冬季运动国际交流合作，与冰雪运动强国组织开展交流活动。

二、建设更多优质冰雪场地设施

北京冬奥会筹办以来，中国冰雪场地数量大幅增加。截至 2021 年初，全国已有 654 块标准冰场，较 2015 年增加 317%，已有 803 个室内外各类滑雪场，较 2015 年增加 41%，为推广普及冰雪运动提供了坚实的硬件保障。未来，中国将通过充分挖掘现有冰雪场地资源存量、因地制宜建设更多优质冰雪场地、持续提升服务保障水平、持续推动残疾人冰雪运动场地建设等方式，为广大民众参与冰雪运动提供更大便利。

充分挖掘现有场地资源。继续盘活存量资源，鼓励场馆多元化利用，增加冰雪场地设施供给，同时因地制宜建设多样化冰雪场地设施。结合现有体育场馆设施，建设综合性冰雪运动中心。支持现有条件的滑雪场进行改扩建增容，完善设施功能，提升服务水平。鼓励通过改造旧厂房、仓库、老旧商业设施等建设室内冰雪运动场地。

因地制宜建设冰雪场地设施。持续鼓励各地合理利用江河、湖泊等自然水域资源和城市公园的公开水域等，开辟天然滑冰场地。依托气候、地貌和生态等自然资源因地制宜建设滑雪场地。鼓励公共体育场地、社区广场及有条件的学校采用多种方式延续设立季节性、临时性、可拆装式冰雪场地，满足学校教学、课外活动及社区居民休闲娱乐需要。加快推进在学校、公园、体育中心、旅游景点、商业综合体等地建设旱雪场、旱冰场、仿真冰场、可拆装冰场等替代性冬季运动场地。

新建优质冰雪场地设施。科学规划冰雪场地设施布局，鼓励有条件的地区将群众冬季运动场地纳入当地土地利用总体规划、城镇化和新农村建设规划。有计划地新建一批滑冰馆、室外滑冰场和滑雪场等冰雪运动场地。继续实施"百城千冰"计划，引导支持配建一批举步可就、经济环保的群众性冰雪场地设施，并纳入全民健身场地设施建设工程统筹。

持续推动残疾人冰雪运动场地设施建设。高度重视残疾人冬季健身场地设施和无障碍建设需求，配备适合残疾

● 2022年1月在辽宁沈阳浑河冰面上举办中国·沈阳第4届冰龙舟大赛暨第2届冰帆大赛

● 四川建成大型室内滑雪场

中国冰雪场地设施增长情况（2015-2021年）

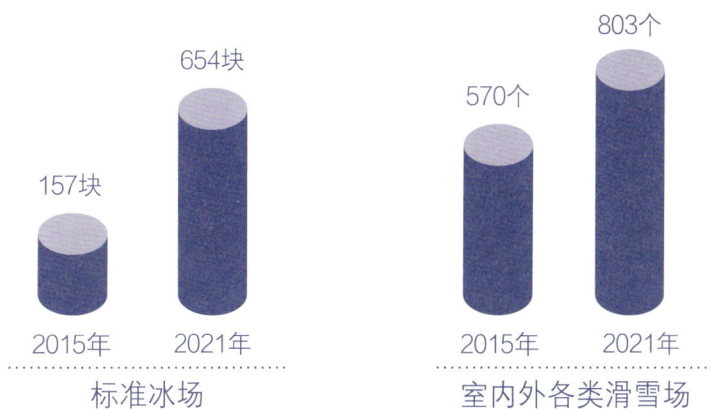

157块
2015年

654块
2021年

标准冰场

570个
2015年

803个
2021年

室内外各类滑雪场

人群体使用的设施设备，开展场地设施的无障碍化改造。研发推出适合残疾人广泛参与的模拟冰雪项目，指导残疾人科学有序开展冰雪活动。冬奥场馆积极服务于残疾人冬季运动发展，坚持永久保留使用无障碍设施遗产。

提升冰雪场地服务保障水平。深入完善冰雪设施建设标准，以标准推动冰雪运动场所建设，加强场地设施、器材装备、从业人员安全规范等方面标准化建设。不断提升冰雪设施服务水平，规范冰雪场地管理，拓展服务项目，扩大公共服务范围。对冰雪场馆免费或低收费开放给予支持。实现冰雪场馆的智能化管理，打造人性、高效、智能的数字冰雪场馆。

● 北京绿心公园举办冰雪嘉年华活动

12
↑
13

三、全面提升冰雪运动竞技水平

北京冬奥会有力地促进了中国冰雪运动竞技水平的大幅提升，以冬奥备战为牵引，通过固强补弱、优化项目布局、科学训练、强化梯队建设等方式多措并举，实现"全项目建队""全项目训练""全项目参赛"，中国体育代表团在冬奥会和冬残奥会均获得了历史最好成绩。中国健儿的精彩表现和夺目的竞技成绩也助推冰雪运动受到全民关注，带动更多民众走进冰场和雪场。未来中国将持续推进冰雪运动项目全面发展，强化后备人才培养，通过提升冰雪运动竞技水平，持续带动更多民众参与冰雪运动。

推进冰雪运动项目全面发展。从项目开展上，促进冰雪运动项目均衡发展，巩固扩展短道速滑等优势项目的技术水平，加大冰球等落后项目的支持力度，科学规划北欧两项等新开展项目。从地域分布上，针对项目特点和地区优势，在不同地区有针对性发展合适的冰雪运动项目。鼓励东北三省开展更多的冰雪项目，加快华北和西北等地冰雪项目发展速度，调动其他有条件的地区开展适宜的冰雪项目。加强区域合作和资源共享，推动冰雪运动跨区域发展。

完善冰雪运动后备人才培养体系。完善以各类各级体校、体育学院和专业队为主，以大中小学校和企业、社会体育组织为辅的多元化人才培养体系，逐步建立年龄层次衔接、项目结构多元、训练规模合理的后备人才队伍。同时，充分发挥竞赛选拔作用，发现和培养一批竞技冰雪运动后备人才。加强高水平后备人才基地的建设，改善后备人才培养的训练设施和师资条件。

促进残疾人竞技冰雪运动持续发展。北京冬残奥会带

北京市通州区潞城全民健身中心

位于北京城市副中心的潞城全民健身中心预计将于2023年年底开放。潞城全民健身中心总建筑面积约为4.8万平方米，被定位为组团级公共体育设施，包括全民健身馆、篮球馆、游泳滑冰馆、网球馆等四大室内场馆，以及约1万平方米的室外运动场地。市民可以在此进行篮球、网球、足球、武术、游泳、滑冰等体育活动，能够满足周边半径3公里内、约5万居民的日常健身休闲及文体活动需求。

● 中国运动员韩聪、隋文静在北京冬奥会花样滑冰双人滑比赛中

动残疾人冬季运动项目在全国开展，全面拓展了残疾人冰雪运动的范围，大幅提升了竞技运动水平。下一步中国将持续推动残疾人冰雪运动发展和竞技水平提升，建立残疾人运动员业余训练体系，加强后备人才培养。建设残疾人体育训练基地，培养残疾人体育教练员、裁判员、分级员等专业人才队伍。同时，继续聘请国外高水平教练团队，选拔优秀运动员组建国家队，力争获得更多的比赛荣誉。

● 中国轮椅冰壶队在比赛中

● 冰雪运动社会指导员指导小朋友滑雪

四、加强冰雪运动人才培养

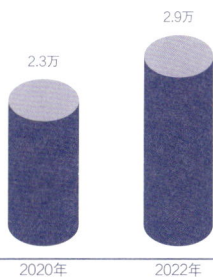

北京市冰雪运动社会指导员人数

在北京冬奥会筹办带动下，中国各类冰雪运动专业人才和基层队伍不断扩大，为冰雪运动普及发展奠定了坚实基础。截至 2022 年 6 月，北京市冰雪运动社会指导员已达到 2.9 万人。北京冬奥会后，中国将继续推动各类冰雪运动人才的培养，加强冰雪运动社会体育指导员队伍建设，加大各类冰雪专业人才培养力度，强化各类冰雪运动培训，不断壮大冰雪运动人才队伍，为中国冰雪运动持续健康发展提供有力人才支撑。

加强冰雪运动社会体育指导员队伍建设。将冰雪运动项目社会体育指导员纳入国家社会体育指导员制度体系，同时将冰雪运动知识和技能培训融入社会体育指导员全员培训体系中。科学建立考核评价机制，培养一批专业素质好、技能水平高、教学能力强的冰雪运动社会体育指导员。

完善标准
为黑龙江建设冰雪运动强省提供支撑

2022年1月29日，黑龙江省发布《滑雪场所（高山）等级划分》，该标准是黑龙江省针对冰雪运动场地设施发布的一项重要地方标准。

《滑雪场所（高山）等级划分》以国家标准《体育场所开放条件与技术要求第6部分：滑雪场所》所规定的相关内容为基础，以滑雪场客运设备数量、基础服务设施设置、滑雪装备数量、机械设备配备、服务人员数量为主要划分依据，将滑雪场所（高山）依次划分为"Ⅰ、Ⅱ、Ⅲ"三个等级。经过等级划分后，不同等级的滑雪场适合承办何种类型、级别的滑雪赛事，以及提供何种类型的冰雪运动服务将更加明确，同时为滑雪爱好者选择适合自己的滑雪体验和消费多了一份参考。该标准的发布实施，为今后黑龙江省乃至全国高山滑雪场所进行场地建设和提供标准化服务提供了标准支撑，也为冰雪产业快速健康发展提供了引领和保障。

● 2022年7月，黑龙江省哈尔滨市的中小学生在气膜冰上运动中心内练习滑冰

● 北京市延庆区普通民众经过技能培训后转型成为浇冰车驾驶员

　　加大冰雪运动各类人才培养力度。鼓励相关高等院校增设冬季运动相关专业或课程，建立冬季运动培训基地、冬季运动研究中心，广泛开展针对性强、专业度高的培训活动。推动冰雪赛事策划与组织、冰雪产业管理、冰雪运动设施维护管理、冰雪运动防护康复等管理型、应用型、技能型人才培养，满足群众性冰雪运动开展需要。借助各类冰雪赛事活动，培养赛事组织人才。

　　丰富冰雪运动人才培训形式。推进冬季运动人才培养体系标准化建设，构建以职业技能鉴定为依托的冬季运动人才评价工作机制，规范技能标准开发、教学培训组织、人员资质认定等相关工作。加大对社会培训机构的扶持力度，利用多样化教育资源，开展冰雪运动培训。采取线上线下相结合的方式，组织开展大众冰雪运动专业技术培训活动，引入国际先进专业培训课程，为冰雪运动参与人群提供更加丰富的技术培训与专业服务。

● 中国滑冰协会主席李琰在"植根计划"活动中带领学员滑冰

五、加强冰雪运动社会组织建设

北京冬奥会申办成功以来，中国冰雪运动社会组织发展迅速，在营造冰雪运动氛围、冰雪运动推广普及、服务冰雪运动爱好者等方面发挥了积极作用。截至2021年12月，中国正式注册的各级冰雪运动社会组织共792个，其中国家级协会8个、省级协会32个、其他冰雪运动社会组织752个，是2015年冰雪运动社会组织数量的2.89倍。随着社会大众对冰雪运动各类需求的不断增长，未来中国将持续培育冬季运动社会组织发展，推动国家冬季运动体育单项协会改革创新，建立多元化的群众性冬季运动体育社团，充分发挥冰雪运动社会组织作用，推动冰雪运动蓬勃有序发展。

培育、扶持冬季运动社会组织发展。完善以体育总会为枢纽，以冰雪运动单项、行业和人群体育协会为支撑，以基层体育社会组织为主体的体育社会组织网络。充分发挥各级

● 中国滑雪协会在陕西西安某小学带领学生跳动冰雪运动健身操

截至2021年12月

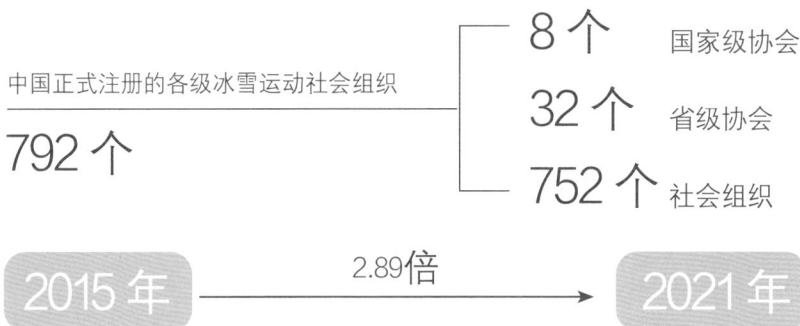

中国正式注册的各级冰雪运动社会组织

792 个

┌ **8 个** 国家级协会
├ **32 个** 省级协会
└ **752 个** 社会组织

2015 年 ——— 2.89倍 ——→ 2021 年

截至2021年12月，中国正式注册的各级冰雪运动社会组织是2015年冰雪运动社会组织数量的2.89倍。

体育总会、冰雪运动协会和其他社会组织的作用，壮大各级各类冬季运动项目协会队伍，激发冬季运动社会组织的发展活力，带动各级各类单项、行业和人群体育组织开展冰雪活动，推动冰雪社会组织创建更多自主品牌赛事和活动。

推动国家冬季运动单项协会创新发展。逐步推动国家各冬季运动单项协会进行实体化改革，探索强化和扩充其在群众体育、体育文化等方面的功能、机制，充分发挥其在群众体育、体育文化发展方面的作用，扩大社会影响力。目前，中国滑冰协会、中国花样滑冰协会、中国冰球协会已实现实体化、市场化运作，下一步，将择机逐步推进中国滑雪协会、中国冰壶协会、中国冬季两项运动协会、中国雪车协会、中国雪橇协会的实体化工作。

建立多元化群众性冬季运动体育社团。鼓励地方冬季运动协会发展俱乐部会员和个人会员，积极发挥不同类型群众性冬季运动体育社会组织的作用，并逐步完成冬季项目体育社会组织的网络化和制度化建设，支持其在社区、乡镇开展活动。

中国滑冰协会推出"植根计划"

2020年1月，为打牢行业根基，中国滑冰协会推出了"植根计划"，目前计划正顺利持续开展。"植根计划"通过开展大众参与度高的"俱乐部公开赛＋训练营＋培训"的模式，开展面向基层滑冰教练员、指导员、学员、裁判员的人才培养，"植根计划"的实施保证了培训的体系化和科学化，切实提高了基层俱乐部基础训练水准，扩大了基层人才储备，为滑冰项目的可持续发展打下了坚实基础。

"植根计划"首先将从增加俱乐部数量方面着手，中国滑冰协会计划在5-7年中、在全国范围内培育一千个滑冰俱乐部。在此基础上，通过专业教练的大量投入，打造高水平、品牌化的俱乐部滑冰公开赛事训练营。在培训方面，训练营中特别注重标准基本功和技术创新、身体素质全面开发、心理健康的教育引导、营养饮食指导、伤病防护和急救知识等方面的培训工作。

"植根计划"计划通过5年植根期，到2024年全运会和2026年冬奥会时，每个省市都能产生高水平滑冰人才，同时使每个参与者都成为滑冰项目未来发展的中坚力量。

● 中国滑冰协会组织开展"植根计划"现场培训

第二章

传承利用奥运场馆遗产转化成为推动发展的新动能

　　北京冬奥会各场馆在建设改造之初就充分考虑场馆的赛后用途，既注重满足赛时需求，又提前谋划场馆的赛后利用。北京冬奥会使用的12个竞赛场馆中，有4个利用了北京2008年奥运会场馆。通过充分借鉴它们的赛后利用经验，所有竞赛场馆和主要非竞赛场馆全部制订了场馆赛后利用计划，通过统筹规划、同步设计，有效降低了未来的再利用成本，促进了场馆的可持续利用。赛时，这些造型优美的场馆充分体现了中国传统文化与奥林匹克元素的完美结合，展示了中国建设者们的匠心独运和高超建筑艺术。赛后，各场馆将推进落实场馆赛后利用计划，申办和举办高水平赛事，面向公众开放，拓展四季运营，助力城市和区域长期可持续发展，实现场馆的"反复利用、综合利用、持久利用"，成为值得传承、造福人民的优质资产。

12个
北京冬奥会
竞赛场馆

4个
利用北京2008年
奥运会场馆

● 首都体育馆

一、积极申办和承办高水平体育赛事

北京冬奥会各竞赛场馆都达到了国际顶级比赛水准，一流的场馆需要一流的赛事作为支撑。在北京冬奥会筹办和举办过程中，各场馆业主与国家和主办城市体育部门、国际单项体育联合会密切沟通，建立了良好关系。赛后，这些场馆将持续加强与国内外体育组织的合作，继续申办、举办高水平国际和国内赛事，带动大众赛事、全民健身和地方发展。

加强与国内外体育组织合作。加强与各国际单项体育联合会、各国家（地区）单项体育联合会以及国家冬季运动各单项协会的沟通和交流，在申办、举办各类国际、国内及地方性体育赛事的同时，积极吸引国家队、专业运动队训练、青少年培训和人才培养等项目落户冬奥场馆，组织开展运动医学和体育科研等相关交流活动。与世界冰壶联合会、中国冰壶协会达成协议，"世界冰壶学院培训中心"落户"冰立方"。国际滑联世界首个"卓越

● 中国雪橇选手范铎耀在国家雪车雪橇中心进行赛前训练

● 2023—2024赛季国际雪联单板及自由式滑雪大跳台世界杯在首钢滑雪大跳台开赛

中心"落户国家速滑馆，推动滑冰运动在中国乃至世界的推广普及。国家雪车雪橇中心与国际雪车联合会等方面签署《谅解备忘录》，未来将定期举办国际雪车联合会各类赛事和训练营。

积极申办、承办国际体育赛事。积极申办和承办世界杯、世锦赛、洲际杯、亚洲杯、积分赛等国际冰雪赛事，通过举办高水平国际赛事，扩大场馆国内外影响力。同时，以举办国际赛事为契机，推动实现赛事和商业活动之间的良性互动。首钢滑雪大跳台作为世界上第一个永久性保留和使用的滑雪大跳台场馆，将积极申办国际雪联单板及自由式滑雪大跳台世界杯赛事。国家高山滑雪中心积极申办国际雪联高山滑雪世界杯等赛事。

主动承办国内赛事。积极对接国家体育总局冬运中心、国家冬季运动各单项协会，承接全国冬季运动会、全国锦标赛、冠军赛、青少年冬季运动会、青少年U系列联赛等国家和地方性冬季运动赛事，辐射带动周边地区冬季运动赛事和活动开展。国家速滑馆将承办速度滑冰、短道速滑、花样滑冰、冰壶、冰球等各类国内冰上赛事。国家体育馆将承接北京市青少年锦标赛和北京市第2届冬季运动会的冰上项目比赛。

二、稳步推进场馆全面向社会开放

将举办体育赛事与服务大众健身有机结合是场馆赛后

● 北京市青少年运动员备战北京市冬季运动会

● 北京冬奥会后，国家速滑馆（冰丝带）举办公众开放活动

利用的首要任务。目前，所有北京冬奥会竞赛场馆已完成从赛时服务阶段向赛后利用的功能转换，全部面向公众开放，组织开展了形式多样的冬奥项目体验、体育展示、参观游览、网红打卡、展览展示等活动。未来，随着场馆改造工作的逐步完成和场馆功能的逐步完善，冬奥场馆将提供更多形式多样、内容丰富、参与度高、更能满足群众各类健身休闲需求的活动，持续服务全民健身事业的发展，使广大民众享受到冬奥场馆的红利。

调整改造场馆设施，满足开放需求。为使冬奥场馆更好地为大众健身服务，降低使用难度，部分场馆将进行针对性改造调整，在保留未来继续举办专业性赛事的基础上，开发公众易于参与且趣味性高的体验项目，使冬奥场馆从仅能由"超人"（即专业运动员）使用转向"常人"（即普通大众）使用，增加了场馆的受众群体，提升了场馆的使用效率。云顶滑雪公园的U型槽、障碍追逐、坡面障碍、平行大回转等赛道，将通过改造适当降低难度向大众开放。国家雪车雪橇中心在360度螺旋弯北侧预留了大众体验出发口，将赛道垂直落差由121米降至40多米，使大众可在

安全前提下体验"冰上F1"的速度与激情。

推进场馆对社会大众开放。推动场馆向公众开放是实现场馆社会效益的有效途径。冬奥会后，各场馆紧扣功能定位，精心策划冰雪体验项目，组织群众性健身活动，一方面利用公众对于北京冬奥会举办的关注热度，原貌展现冬奥场景，精心打造参观流线，服务民众参观游览需求；另一方面组织开展各类冬奥运动项目体验、培训项目、休闲健身和大众赛事活动，满足广大群众全方位的体验和健

● 北京冬奥会后，国家游泳中心（水立方/冰立方）面向公众开放

身需求。国家游泳中心于 2022 年 4 月 16 日对公众开放，举办"面向大众、双奥朝阳、相约冰壶——冰立方冬奥文化大众体验季"，场馆一经开放即成为北京城区"最热的冰"，开放首日即接待游客 3000 多人次。

开展场馆惠民和公益活动。积极推动冬奥场馆开展惠民活动，降低群众消费成本，激发体育消费热情。扩大参与免费开放活动的场馆数量，同时引导场馆分时段向社会

大众低收费开放。倡导各场馆开启馆校对接，让青少年了解冬季运动项目和奥林匹克文化，组织开展冬奥项目公开课活动。组织专业教练针对不同水平冰雪爱好者设计不同的体验项目，进行技术指导和教学，进一步调动大众参与的积极性。首都体育馆正式发起"冰雪惠民计划"，面向全国冰雪运动场馆发起"每月面向社会不少于1次免费开放"的倡议，并倡议冰雪运动场馆定期面向社会开展各类群众

● 北京冬奥会后，首都体育馆开展公众开放日活动

● 北京冬奥会后，云顶滑雪公园开展儿童暑期阅读夏令营

"冰雪惠民计划"

免费 > 1 次

每月面向社会开放

33 家

首批参与冰场

喜爱、易于参与的公益冰雪课，为广大群众和青少年参与冰雪运动提供便利条件，京津冀地区 33 家冰场成为首批参与"冰雪惠民计划"的体育设施。

三、推动实现场馆四季运营

北京冬奥会后，所有奥运场馆都将打造成为多功能综合体，开展多业态经营，实现四季利用。冰上场馆作为室内场馆，可实现四季向公众开放、举办各类大型赛事和文化休闲活动，雪上场馆在冬季将开展冰雪运动，其他季节将开发各类户外运动、旅游休闲和山地度假等产业，推动实现场馆的四季运营。

持续开展冰雪运动。各场馆结合自身冬季运动项目特点，进行差异化运营，冰上和雪上场馆将分别在全年和冬季因地制宜开展各类冰雪运动，举办冰雪赛事，开展大众冬季健身活动。国家速滑馆拥有 1.2 万平米冰面，将可通过举办冰上赛事和大众体验活动，满足超过 2000 人同时开展速度滑冰、短道速滑、花样滑冰、冰球、冰壶等五大类冰上运动的需求。游客不仅可以租用冰鞋用速度滑冰的方式亲身体验"最快的冰"，也可体验冰上嬉戏等各类大众冰上休闲娱乐活动。

拓展四季运动。北京冬奥会冰上场馆多为双奥场馆，经过改造，增添了冬季运动功能，开启"双轮驱动""四季运转"模式，同步开展夏季运动项目和大众健身活动。延庆和张家口雪上场馆，受气候限制，在冬季将开展雪上项目体验和比赛，在其他季节将充分利用赛区的人文历史和自然生态优势，建立户外拓展训练中心，发展健身跑、越野跑、山地自行车、登山、攀岩、徒步、滑草等户外运动，不断开拓四季运动。国家越野滑雪中心将打造集登山健身、山地骑行、徒步穿越、崖壁攀岩等于一体的山地户外运动公园。

开展多业态经营。除开展各类体育运动外，各场馆还将充分利用赛区生态和旅游资源，发展区域特色旅游休闲、山地度假等产业，促进体育与文化、旅游的融合发展。首钢滑雪大跳台将以氛围照明系统为特色，主打工业遗址风格，承接户外音乐会、新车发布会、音乐节、啤酒节、灯光秀等商业活动。云顶滑雪公园非雪季收入已占全年收入的90%，其特色项目包括观星、儿童夏令营、亲子音乐艺

国家速滑馆

"最快的冰"

A 1.2万平米全亚洲最大冰面

B 可举办5大类冰上运动

C 可满足2000人同时上冰体验

术节等各类亲子休闲主题活动等。国家跳台滑雪中心通过妥善利用出发区和结束区，将举办会议、足球赛和音乐会，同时联合太子城冰雪小镇会议会展中心，组团成为山地会议会展举办地。

四、融入地区整体发展

北京冬奥会秉持场馆规划建设与城市发展规划相统一的理念，这些精心打造的冬奥场馆作为城市发展的支撑要素，将有助于落实城市战略定位，促进体育运动和冰雪产业发展，提升城市文化品质，培育全季旅游目的地，促进生态环境可持续发展，增强城市发展动能。

北京赛区场馆提升"双奥之城"影响力。北京赛区各场馆将紧密服务城市战略定位，通过开展各类品牌赛事活动，服务全民健身和体育事业发展，增强国际间体育和人文交往，打造"双奥之城"国际交往承载地，提升城市形象和文化软实力。国家会议中心二期将举办国务、政务及高端商务会展活动，全部投入使用后将与国家会议中心形成总规模将近130万平方米的会展综合体，成为北京城市会客厅。

延庆赛区场馆助力最美冬奥城建设。延庆赛区将服务延庆区国家全域旅游示范区和国际文化体育旅游休闲名区的功能定位，作为"冬奥、世园、长城"三张金名片的重要组成部分，推动延庆全域旅游发展。作为北部冬奥冰雪消费带的核心，延庆赛区将以"四季、竞技、体验、冬奥"四项元素为内容依托，促进"体育+旅游"深度融合，围绕冰雪健康户外主题,挖掘培育冰雪运动IP,打造冰雪主题、山地旅游融合、四季皆宜度假目的地。延庆赛区已于2022年5月1日正式向公众开放，随着逐步完善，延庆赛区和冬奥场馆设施将为"最美冬奥城"的发展增添强大动力。

张家口赛区场馆助力国际冰雪运动和休闲旅游胜地建设。张家口赛区服务张家口市打造世界级冰雪运动和体育文化旅游目的地的战略定位，服务将崇礼区打造为国际冰雪旅游目的地和高端会议会展中心的核心目标，依托现有旅游、文化和场馆资源，着力引入"赛、会、演、典、展、学、游、健"八大业态，通过"体育＋文旅商养"多业态融合发展，将张家口赛区打造成为集专业赛事、会展节演、康养度假、

● 国家会议中心二期（主媒体中心）赛后举办2022年中国国际服务贸易交易会

● 2022年第2届京张全季体育旅游嘉年华在国家跳台滑雪中心（雪如意）启动

研学培训于一体的世界级"文体旅"目的地。目前，张家口崇礼奥林匹克公园和云顶滑雪公园已对公众开放，并举办"京张全季体育旅游嘉年华"和"越山向海"人车接力赛等群众性体育活动。随着文体旅产品的不断融合和品牌效应的不断提升，张家口赛区对于张家口市国际冰雪运动和休闲旅游胜地建设将发挥持续的带动作用。

冰雪运动在中国的广泛普及，有力推动了冰雪产业的快速发展，初步形成了以冰雪大众健身休闲为主，装备制造、冰雪旅游、竞赛表演、运动培训、场馆服务和冰雪会展等协同发展的产业格局，冰雪健身休闲业蓬勃发展，装备制造创新能力不断增强，冰雪旅游持续拉动冰雪消费，有力带动了冰雪产业加速崛起。中国冰雪产业总规模从2015年的2700亿元增长至2020年的6000亿元。冬奥会后，中国将持续推动冰雪产业升级发展，优化产业布局，完善产业发展体系，不断提升自主研发能力，推动冰雪产业全面协调可持续发展，预计到2025年，中国冰雪产业总规

中国冰雪产业总规模

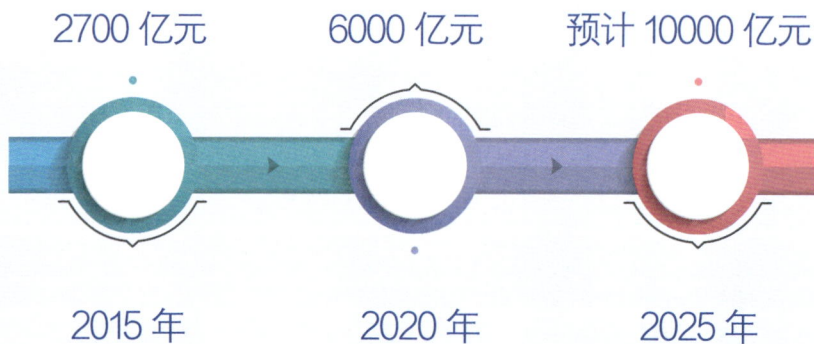

2700 亿元	6000 亿元	预计 10000 亿元
2015 年	2020 年	2025 年

● 2022年服贸会体育板块上展示的浇冰车

模达到 10000 亿元。

一、做实冰雪装备制造业

以冬奥筹办为契机，中国冰雪运动装备制造业跨越一道道技术难关，产品从无到有，品牌从有到优，市场规模与投资力度不断扩大，产业园区蓬勃兴起，自主研发能力逐步增强，冰雪装备市场消费大幅增长，装备制造业发展步入快车道。截至 2020 年，全国各地冰雪装备器材产业园区及小镇接近 20 个；2022 年，中国冰雪装备器材产业预计年销售收入将超过 200 亿元人民币，年均增速 20% 以上。冰雪装备制造是冰雪产业的发展基础，后冬奥时期，将加快培育冰雪装备制造产业，不断提升供给能力，打造一批具有国际竞争力的国产品牌，推动创建一批特色产业园区，形成具备高质量发展基础的冰雪装备产业体系。

进一步优化冰雪装备制造产业布局。深入实施冰雪装备器材产业发展行动计划，加强战略规划布局，持续在东北、华北地区发展冰雪机械装备制造业，进一步提升长三角、珠三角、海峡西岸等体育产业集群在冰雪器材装备研发生产方面的能力。优化产业结构，着力开发大众冰雪装备器材，实施精品装备制造示范应用工程，鼓励高科技冰雪运动装备研发，打造冰雪智能运动装备一体化产业链。

进一步加强冰雪装备制造产业基地建设。推动冰雪产业基地发展，有条件的地区打造一批冰雪装备制造特色产业园区，加快产业聚集，提升设计研发、生产制造、现代

● 张家口冰雪产业园

服务等全产业链发展水平，发挥示范引领和辐射带动作用。河北省廊坊市加快冰雪产业强市建设步伐，布局工业园区建设，重点培育引进冰雪装备制造产业落地，加快形成"冰雪运动、冰雪装备研发制造、冰雪旅游、人才培养、冰雪文化"为核心的冰雪全产业链条。吉林市冰雪装备产业园重点引进一批索道缆车、造雪机等重型设备生产企业和碳纤维滑雪板、滑雪服等轻装备生产企业，计划投资3亿元，占地面积10万余平米。

持续提升冰雪装备制造自主研发创新能力。以"科技冬奥"为引领，以技术创新促产业升级，不断加强原创性技术和核心技术创新，提升本土冰雪企业自主研发能力，面向国内外市场，打造冰雪产品高端品牌，进一步提升国产化率和市场占有率。引进国外先进的制造技术与国内研发并进，不断提升高端配套零部件自制率。推进科研院所、高等院校和企业科研力量优化配置和资源共享。

二、做大冰雪旅游业

北京冬奥会带动冰雪旅游业快速增长，冰雪旅游成为全民新时尚，旅游人数和旅游收入大幅增加，旅游企业和投资数额不断扩大，冰雪小镇和冰雪旅游度假区蓬勃发展，冰雪旅游市场潜能进一步激发。2020—2021雪季全国冰雪旅游人数达2.3亿人次，旅游收入达到3900亿。冰雪旅游是促进内需、带动消费的重要一环，冬奥会后，将继续利用好冬奥冰雪资源，持续推动冰雪旅游市场健康快速发展，打造一批高品质冰雪主题旅游度假区和滑雪旅游度假地。

　　丰富冰雪旅游产品供给。依托丰富的冬奥冰雪场馆资源，打造一批有影响力的冰雪旅游精品线路、精品赛事和示范基地，将北京延庆区和张家口崇礼区打造成为世界知名的滑雪旅游度假胜地，促进国家级体育旅游示范区建设。支持各地建设一批交通便利、基础设施完善、冰雪景观独

● 北京冬奥会闭幕后吉林长春百姓上冰雪的热情不减

特、产品服务优质、冰雪风情浓郁的冰雪主题省级旅游度
假区，推出一批兼具民俗风情和冰雪文化特色的冰雪旅游
主题精品线路，大力拓展冰雪竞赛表演市场，引导培育冰
雪运动商业表演项目，大力发展乡村冰雪旅游，推动建设
雪乡、雪村、雪庄、雪镇，丰富冰雪旅游供给。北京市积

极支持西部新首钢地区打造北京冬季奥林匹克公园，开发新型工业旅游，加快建设成为集专业体育竞技、时尚运动精品与高端服务业于一体的体育产业示范区，依托北部北京奥林匹克公园，大力发展文旅体和会议会展业。

扩大冰雪旅游消费潜力。面向国际和国内两个市场，培育塑造冰雪旅游品牌，加强对冰雪旅游、冰雪文化和冰雪运动的宣传和展示，引导人民群众积极参与冰雪旅游活动。培养市场主体，优化消费环境，鼓励和引导各地结合本地市场需求，推动冰雪设施与文化、商业、娱乐等综合开发，打造冰雪旅游服务综合体，促进冰雪旅游消费，探索设立各具特色的地方"冰雪日"。2022年7月，河北省举办第2届"京张全季旅游嘉年华"，以体育旅游为引领，全面提升京张体育文化旅游带的体验性、知名度和影响力。

推动冰雪旅游融合发展。促进"冰雪旅游＋文化"融合，挖掘利用冬奥冰雪文化资源和各地传统冰雪文化资源，丰富冰雪旅游文

● 黑龙江省哈尔滨市冰雪大世界

● 2022年7月25日，北京西山永定河文化节在首钢三高炉开幕

化元素和节庆冰雪活动，打造冰雪文化旅游季。促进"冰雪旅游＋教育"融合，依托冬奥场馆和冰雪资源，积极与学校开展合作，推广普及青少年冰雪运动，推动冰雪研学旅游和冬令营发展。促进"冰雪旅游＋科技"融合，大力发展互联网上的冰雪旅游，综合应用"科技冬奥"成果，加快推动大数据、云计算、物联网、区块链及5G、北斗系统、虚拟现实等新技术在旅游领域的应用普及，推动智慧旅游发展。

三、做强冰雪竞赛表演业

北京冬奥会极大地带动了冰雪赛事的蓬勃发展，各类冰雪赛事表演活动数量稳步增长，有力地推动了冬季运动项目普及，服务群众性赛事活动和地方经济的发展。自2015年以来，速度滑冰、冰球、冰壶、单板及自由式滑雪大跳台等国际高级别冰雪赛事纷纷落户中国，全国各地单板滑雪、花样滑冰、短道速滑等具有较强观赏性的精品冰雪赛事数量持续增加。各类青少年冰雪赛事方兴未艾，有效推动了各类国内、国际专业冰雪体育赛事升级发展。冬奥会后，我们将持续推动冰雪竞赛表演业繁荣发展，依托

● 2023—2024赛季国际滑联短道速滑世界杯北京站在首都体育馆举行

● 第13届全国冬运会在新疆乌鲁木齐举行

冬奥场馆打造冰雪赛事高地，将国际赛事与国内赛事、专业赛事与大众赛事、体育赛事与大众健身有机结合，持续服务带动大众健身休闲和竞技体育发展。

积极举办国际高水平冰雪赛事。加强与国际奥委会、国际单项体育联合会等国际体育组织的交流合作，巩固和提升已有国际赛事的知名度和品牌形象，引进更多国际精品冰雪赛事，积极申办和举办世界杯、世锦赛、洲际杯、冠军杯、大奖赛等国际高级别冬季运动赛事，引进国际健身休闲赛事，鼓励有条件的地区和城市积极申办洲际、青少年和大学生冬季运动会。依托冬奥场馆资源与体育组织建立长期战略合作关系，建设国际体育人才培训中心和高水平运动员训练基地，落户国际冬季运动人才培养项目，依托京张体育文化旅游带建设，打造京津冀国际顶级冰雪赛事活动平台和聚集地，通过国际赛事持续带动地区经济发展和冬季运动项目普及推广。

大力培育国内冰雪赛事表演市场。持续举办好"全国冬季运动会"等综合性冰雪赛事，不断创新形式、丰富内容，合理设置群众性比赛项目和竞赛活动，满足群众参赛和体验需求。鼓励各地持续开展参与度高、普及面广、影响力大、带动性强的冬季项目品牌赛事和活动，发挥对群众性冬季运动的引领、示范、带动作用。在非雪季组织开展轮滑、滑轮、滑草等与冰雪技能相关的赛事活动。推动专业冰雪体育赛事升级发展，吸引全球冰雪运动爱好者，促进冬季项目职业化发展，开展冰球等职业联赛。支持社会力量打造花样滑冰、冰球、冰壶、单板滑雪和短道速滑等观赏性强的精品冰雪赛事，引导培育冰雪运动商业表演项目，不断拓展国内冰雪赛事表演市场。

大力推动青少年冰雪赛事。进一步丰富全国青少年冰雪赛事活动，持续扩大全国青年运动会冬季项目的设置，扩大青少年运动员参赛规模。健全冰雪项目 U 系列赛事品牌，加快体育传统冰雪特色学校建设，持续以赛事引导青少年参与冰雪、热爱冰雪。鼓励高等学校建立高水平冰雪运动队，持续推动赛事社会化，开展青少年俱乐部联赛，巩固特色学校、俱乐部、训练营、校外活动中心等多元化培养模式。2021-2022 北京市青少年冰球俱乐部联赛共进行 1224 场比赛，共有 25 家俱乐部、256 支队伍近 3600 名球员参赛，赛事规模继续保持亚洲第一。

● 中国青少年冰球联赛总决赛暨全国U14冰球锦标赛在山东泰山开赛

第四章

持续发挥奥运带动作用
推动城市高质量发展

　　北京冬奥会的筹办极大地带动了北京、张家口等主办城市的更新和升级发展，全面提升了城市的知名度和影响力，奥林匹克精神深入人心，全民健身热情高涨，社会文明程度显著提升，推动首钢地区、延庆、张家口成为冬奥筹办带动本地发展的典型范例，实现了奥林匹克运动与城市发展的双赢。冬奥会后，将全面发挥奥运遗产对城市发展的促进和带动作用，进一步放大和延长冬奥效应，扩大北京"双奥之城"影响力，打造首钢"首都城市复兴新地标"，建设延庆"最美冬奥城"和张家口"国际冰雪运动和

● 首钢园

60
↗
61

体育文化旅游目的地城市",持久释放遗产效益,为城市的
高质量发展和人民的幸福生活注入永久动力。

一、首钢——首都城市复兴新地标

　　以冬奥筹办为契机,紧抓时代机遇,首钢园区成为城
市工业遗产保护再利用的典范。紧密围绕冬奥服务保障,
加速建成北京冬奥组委办公区、国家队训练基地和首钢滑
雪大跳台等一批冬奥设施和冰雪场馆,建设国家体育产业
示范区;坚持生态优先,活化利用工业遗存,改造释放 54

万平米城市特色发展空间，建设北京冬季奥林匹克公园，推动山、水、冬奥、工业遗存创新融合发展。首钢老工业更新项目获得首届"北京城市更新最佳实践"活动大奖。冬奥会后，首钢园将持续创新探索工业遗存再利用的特色发展之路，加快实施新首钢三年行动计划，建设京西产业转型升级示范区，塑造代表首都形象的重要窗口，深入打造"新时代首都城市复兴新地标"。

进一步发展体育＋产业。用好北京冬奥遗产，走专业化市场化国际化经营之路，充分发挥北京冬奥遗产的溢出效应。利用北京冬奥会为首钢园区打造的以健康乐活为底色的特质，打造极限公园，开展滑板、攀岩等户外极限运动。经营好首钢滑雪大跳台，与国际体育组织合作举办高

● 首钢极限公园

水平国际赛事、认证培训，同时面向社会开放，开展多业态、多元化运营，满足多层次需求。继续经营好短道速滑、花样滑冰、冰壶、冰球四个训练馆，为专业运动队提供训练服务，同时组织开展相关赛事。充分利用服贸会展馆，在闭会期间出租开展室内篮球等培训活动，服务全民健身。

大力培育科技＋产业。顺应北京打造国际科技创新中心的城市战略定位，发挥首钢空间优势，打造集中连片的科技创新空间载体。结合京西和石景山区在游戏、VR、AR领域的产业积累，按照面向未来、面向年轻人、面向国际化的发展思路，着重培育人工智能、科幻、元宇宙三个方面的产业生态，积极围绕新兴产业进行布局。开展人工智能相关示范场景应用，吸引智能驾驶等方面企业和项目入驻；吸引和做好中关村科幻产业创新中心、中国科幻研究中心及相关上下游企业入驻工作；牵头组建好"科幻产业联合体"。

打造宜居宜业园区。在已建成的冬奥广场区等三个片区的基础上，继续按照既定规划，完成后续的城市织补创新工厂区和国际人才社区建设，服务产业发展。建设长安街金轴城市织补创新工场区，继续注重传承工业文化脉络，坚持以人为本，体现小街区密路网、立体慢行交通系统、开放共享交流空间等新理念。国际人才社区增强空间包容性，依托中心城区区位优势，面向国际高端人才、年轻创新创业群体，形成"创新研发＋商务办公＋运动乐活＋品质休闲"多元混合的功能布局，进一步推进区域职住平衡，提升地区可持续发展新活力。

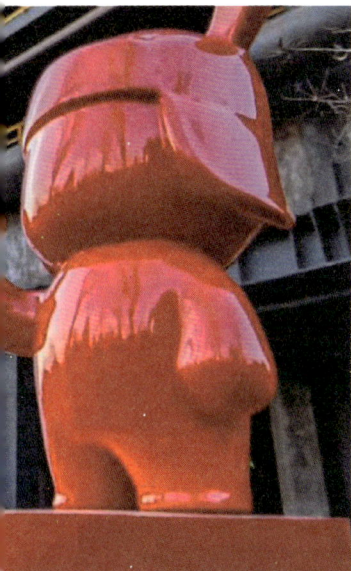

1		5
2	3	6
	4	7
8		

1. 五一剧场　　　　　5. 茶钢儿餐厅

2. 高炉超体空间　　　6. 六工汇商业综合体

3. 全民畅读书店　　　7. 首钢工舍酒店

4. 瞭仓艺术馆　　　　8. 服贸会场地

二、延庆——最美冬奥城

筹办北京冬奥会为延庆的绿色发展奠定基础、带来机遇。基础设施提质升级，京礼高速、京张高铁延庆支线建成通车；冰雪资源加速集聚，延庆奥林匹克园区精彩开园；体育文化旅游产业迅猛发展，建成精品民宿100余家；"冬奥、长城、世园"三张金名片联动发展，城市品牌认知度和影响力与日俱增。未来，延庆将接续冬奥效应、用好冬奥遗产，进一步发展壮大冰雪体育产业，做强做精全域特色旅游产业，持续建设"最美冬奥城"，奋力谱写"冰雪新篇章"。

持续擦亮城市金名片。北京冬奥会给延庆留下了国家高山滑雪中心、国家雪车雪橇中心等一批世界一流的场馆

● 初冬飞雪扮靓延庆世园美景

● 北京冬奥会火炬台永久矗立延庆冬奥城市文化广场

设施和"延庆奥林匹克园区"的品牌资产,这些有形和无形的奥运遗产都是促进地区发展的宝贵财富。为扩大和延续冬奥效应,赛后,延庆赛区将持续申办、举办高山滑雪、雪车雪橇等国内外高水平体育赛事,同时,推动冬奥场馆和赛区全面对公众开放,开发适合大众的冰雪运动体验项目,建设大众雪场等配套设施,服务不同级别的滑雪爱好者参与冰雪运动。在非雪季,将充分利用人文历史和自然生态优势,大力发展山地度假、旅游休闲、户外运动,实现场馆的四季运营,将延庆奥林匹克园区打造成为具有国际影响力的休闲度假和冰雪旅游目的地。此外,通过举办高端节庆活动、展览会议、冰雪活动和民俗文化活动等,将冬奥文化、世园文化、长城文化与"美丽延庆冰雪夏都"城市品牌建设充分融合，擦亮城市金名片。

发展壮大冰雪体育产业。北京冬奥会推动了京张体育文化旅游带的建设和发展，作为其中的重要一核，延庆逐步释放出冰雪产业的发展潜力。后冬奥时期，延庆将持续普及推广冰雪运动，丰富冰雪设施供给，扩建万科石京龙滑雪场，在八达岭滑雪场新增"嬉雪乐园"，带动更多群众参与冰雪运动。充分发挥北京国际奥林匹克学院教学资源和优势，创建全国校园冰雪运动试点区，加强冰雪运动人才培养和文化传播。加快中关村（延庆）体育科技前沿技

● 延庆石京龙滑雪场

● 北京延庆奥林匹克园区

术创新中心建设，加大冰雪产业发展的政策扶持力度，推动体育产业上下游的发展，逐步形成冰雪产业生态圈。通过促进冰雪运动与旅游、教育、科技等产业深度融合，逐步完善冰雪产业链。

做强做精旅游附加产业。在北京冬奥会带动下，延庆知名度迅速提升，全域旅游加速发展，成功创建全域旅游示范区。未来将继续延伸旅游附加产业链条，提升服务和产品品质，带动群众增收致富。继续重点培育"冬奥人家""世园人家""长城人家""山水人家"等特色品牌民宿产业，到"十四五"末，预计打造精品民宿品牌150个、建成民宿小院600个。改造传统餐饮街区，提升延庆美食旅游知名度和吸引力。做精延庆礼物品牌，策划推出"冬奥礼物""世园礼物""长城礼物""妫川礼物"等系列特色文化旅游产品。启动旅游商品"后备箱"工程，包装林果、蔬菜、畜牧、杂粮等地方特产，推动"妫水农耕"品牌农产品向旅游商品转化。

三、张家口——国际冰雪运动和体育文化旅游目的地城市

北京冬奥会的筹办带动张家口市在基础设施、产业转型、生态环境、城乡面貌、民生福祉等各项事业发展中取得显著成效，为张家口全面提速发展打下了坚实基础。未来，张家口市将以建设京张体育文化旅游带为龙头，以冬

特色品牌民宿业

冬奥人家

世园人家

长城人家

山水人家

到2025年

打造精品民俗品牌
150 个

建成民宿小院
600 个

奥场馆赛后利用为牵引，以文旅深度融合发展为主攻方向，以冰雪经济为特色，以可再生能源示范区建设为重要抓手，把奥运遗产转化为推动创新绿色发展的新动能，加快高质量发展步伐，书写好后奥运发展的新篇章。

推动冬奥场馆赛后利用。北京冬奥会为张家口留下了云顶滑雪公园、古杨树场馆群、张家口冬奥村和颁奖广场等一大批竞赛和非竞赛场馆设施。下一步，将深入实施场馆赛后利用计划，完善基础设施和配套服务，推动场馆与地区联动发展，丰富商业、教育、科技、文化、旅游、度假等功能，集中精力打造崇礼世界级冰雪运动目的地，培育壮大赛事经济、会展经济、论坛经济、研学经济，实现场馆四季运营和冬奥遗产利用效益最大化。

推动冰雪经济做大做强。以冬奥筹办为契机，张家口立足冰雪资源优势和产业发展基础，以冰雪装备研发制造为重点，在高新区和宣化区建设了2个各占地3000多亩的冰雪产业园。未来，将实施2个冰雪产业园区的能级提升工程，加大产业链招商、以商招商力度，培育全产业链条，打造世界级冰雪运动高地和冰雪产业集聚区。

推动文旅深度融合发展。张家口拥有丰富的文化和旅游资源，京张高铁和京礼高速的开通运营联通了北京这个

● 张家口城市夜景

巨大的客源市场，也使大量游客可以快速到达张家口。赛后，将实施景区景点提档升级和文旅品牌创建培育工程，推进京张跨区域项目建设和景区运营，深化全域旅游创建，为经济社会发展注入新的活力。目前，围绕京张体育文化旅游带建设谋划储备项目达652个，首批46个项目已开工。

着力构建绿色产业体系。冬奥筹办带动了张家口可再生能源产业的发展，推动建立了区域绿电交易机制，打通绿电输送、存储和消费全链条，形成了光伏、风电、氢能、大数据产业在内的"可再生能源＋产业"的发展模式。未来，将继续结合可再生能源示范区建设，以储能攻坚为重点推进风光储一体化；加快推进氢能产业创新中心、高密度储氢重大战略产业基地等一批重点项目建设，打造国家级氢能产业示范城市和氢能源制备基地；结合建设"东数西算"国家数据中心集群，以应用攻坚为重点提升数字经济整体发展水平。同时，将强化要素保障和政策供给，提升项目建设质效，带动产业转型升级。

● 张北云计算数据中心

72

73

" "

张家口三大主题旅游线路

冬奥冰雪激情之旅：主要串联崇礼冬奥场馆群（国家跳台滑雪中心等）、滑雪场群、张北塞那都冰雪世界、沽源库伦淖尔旅游度假区、尚义鸳鸯湖滑雪场等景区景点，并积极将沿线赤城海坨山谷旅游度假区、赤城温泉度假村、沽源滦河神韵景区、沽水福源度假村、张北德胜民俗村、野狐岭军事要塞旅游区、尚义大青山景区、十三号村等景区景点纳入其中。

历史文化体验之旅：主要串联怀来鸡鸣驿城、黄龙山庄、下花园鸡鸣山、宣化古城、桥西大境门、张家口堡、万全右卫城等景区景点。

生态人文研学之旅：主要串联怀来世界葡萄酒之窗、官厅水库国家湿地公园、怀来葡萄酒庄、丁玲纪念馆、涿鹿黄帝城遗址、蔚县暖泉古镇、蔚州博物馆、小五台·金河口景区、阳原泥河湾国家遗址公园、宣化桑干河大峡谷等景区景点。

● 河北怀来鸡鸣驿古城

张家口赛区

草原天路　　　　大境门

延庆赛区

八达岭长城　　　北京世园公园　　百里画廊

图例

= = = = = = = = = =
京礼高速

- - - - - - - - - -
京藏高速

+ + + + + + + + +
京张高铁

● 京张体育文化旅游带示意图

城遗址公园

故宫

天坛

颐和园

京赛区

第五章

加快建设京张体育文化旅游带

有序推进京津冀协同发展

北京冬奥会对于京张体育文化旅游带的建设起到了强有力的推动作用。在打造北京、延庆、张家口这三个位于带状区域核心节点位置的赛区时，注重将当地体育资源和文化旅游资源相结合，通过京张高铁和京礼高速的建设和运营使沿途各地快速相连，并在生态环境、产业发展、公共服务等方面加强共建共享和协同保障，使冬奥筹办有力促进区域体育、文化、旅游的融合发展，京张体育文化旅游带建设初见成效。北京冬奥会后，为利用好京张体育文化旅游带建设这个促进京津冀协同发展的重要抓手，国家和京冀两地相继出台系列发展规划，相关措施持续深入实施。未来，将充分利用冬奥遗产，强化区域协同和支撑体系建设，推进体育、文化和旅游多产业创新融合，打造京张体育文化旅游协同发展新高地，为京津冀协同发展注入新活力。

一、推进区域体育事业快速发展

在北京冬奥会的带动下，京张地区大力普及推广冰雪运动，建设了一批世界一流的奥运场馆和冰雪设施，冰雪赛事活动蓬勃开展，这些为区域体育事业发展奠定了重要基础。未来，京张体育文化旅游带建设将以奥运场馆为核心，进一步打造赛事会展聚集地、建设全民健身引领地、培育创新发展新场景，推动区域体育产业发展迈向新高度。

丰富赛事活动，提高奥运场馆利用效率。打造重要赛事活动集聚地。提升赛事活动举办和服务水平，推动奥运场馆承接国内外各级各类冰雪竞技赛事，着力打造服务全国、辐射世界的顶级赛事集聚地。建设冰雪运动训练基地。引进国际一流冰雪人才培训项目，优化冰雪人才队伍，加强与国内外知名体育机构交流合作，加大冰雪运动人才培训力度，加快冰雪运动培训体系建设，打造延庆、崇礼国家综合训练基地。积极举办区域赛事活动。以"赛城融合"为理念，塑造"一县（区）一品"体育赛事活动品牌，开展各类冰雪品牌赛事和特色体育赛事活动，构建"专业赛事＋原创赛事"的精品赛事体系。打造会展活动新高地。充分发挥京张两地龙头骨干企业的引领带动作用和重大功能性平台集聚作用，举办一批具有国际影响力的会展活动，打造具有全球影响力的国际交流平台和高端会展活动新高地。

推进全民健身，完善大众健身公共服务体系建设。推广普及冰雪运动。建立健全冰雪运动发展政策体系，推广普及青少年冰雪运动项目，开展公益冰雪运动体验、欢乐冰雪季等群众性冰雪活动，建设"带动三亿人参与冰雪运动"示范区。拓展全季体育运动。鼓励引入季节性、临时性体育和文化娱乐体验项目，支持现有公园因地制宜增加体育设施，鼓励有条件的地方建设辐射面大、设施完善、功能健全的体育公园。优化全民健身服务供给。积极推动奥运场馆服务提升，拓展体育赛事、群众健身、文化休闲、展览展示、社会公益等功能，支持打造一批特色鲜明、功能完善、效益良好的体育服务综合体，加快建设一批有影响力的国家体育产业示范基地。

深化创新合作，助力区域体育产业协同发展。建设奥运文化传播窗口。支持符合条件的奥运场馆建设奥运展览馆，加快推进北京冬季奥林匹克公园、延庆奥林匹克园区、张家口崇礼奥林匹克公园建设，加快建设北京国际奥林匹克学院。提升奥运场馆使用效率。推动奥运场馆赛后低碳运行，将场馆由单一的体育功能拓展为集体育、文化、旅游和休闲娱乐的综合体，深化奥运场馆体制机制改革。打造创新创意新场景。依托5G、8K超高清视频、VR/AR、大数据、云计算、人工智能等现代科技，推动奥运场馆智慧化建设，提升智能化水平。带动周边区域发展。支持延庆区、崇礼区以奥运场馆为核心，加快发展区域特色旅游休闲等产业，建设集运动、休闲、会议、度假为一体的高品质休闲度假地。

● **亚洲单体最大综合性冰上中心——北京市冰上项目训练基地在延庆落成**

❝ 京津冀品牌赛（节）事

打造户外山野健身休闲品牌赛（节）事。开展京津冀三地马拉松赛、徒步登山赛、环京津冀（或运动休闲带）活力三项比赛（徒步、跑步、自行车）、环京津冀自行车赛等赛（节）事。开展京冀草原天路超级马拉松赛、京张长城超级旅跑国际赛、京津冀国际自行车拉力赛、康宝草原国际马拉松等大型赛事活动。

打造民族民间体育品牌赛（节）事。开展京津冀三地风筝节、京津冀武术节、京津冀龙舟比赛、京津冀空竹艺术节、沧州武术节、踢毽子比赛等活动。

打造现代竞技体育品牌赛（节）事。开展京津冀三地篮球、排球、足球、羽毛球、乒乓球、网球、气排球、科技航模、铁人三项赛（依托天津铁人三项赛）、赛车等现代竞技体育赛事。

打造冰雪运动品牌赛（节）事。开展京津冀三地冰球比赛、雪地马球比赛，举办京张承冰雪嘉年华、"大好河山激情张家口"冰雪季等赛（节）事。

● 2023年1月7日，中国银行Visa信用卡杯超级定点滑雪公开赛在新疆开赛

二、共筑新时代区域文化发展高地

北京冬奥会促进了奥林匹克文化在中国的传播，向世界全面展示了中国优秀传统文化和城市文化特色，同时也将京张体育文化旅游带厚重而悠久的历史、绚丽而丰富的文化展现在全球观众面前。赛后，将通过京张体育文化旅游带建设，持续深入推动奥林匹克文化、中国传统文化、冰雪文化、长城文化等多元文化融合，打造文化名片，搭建文化交流平台，走出文化创新发展新模式。

打造国际文化奥运名城，传播中国文化品牌。打造国际奥运文化名城。拓展北京奥林匹克公园和北京冬季奥林匹克公园文化旅游功能，深化与历届冬奥会举办城市交流与务实合作，提升"双奥之城"国际影响力。建设长城国家文化公园。利用好"长城脚下的奥运会"品牌，与长城国家文化公园建设保护联动发展，统筹以延庆八达岭、张家口大境门和崇礼长城为核心的不同段落长城的保护利用，深入挖掘长城精神内涵、文化价值和景观价值，促进奥运文化与长城文化融合发展。培育百年京张文化品牌。加强对京张铁路沿线历史遗迹、红色文化、工业遗址等重要文化遗产资源的保护与创新利用，加快京张铁路遗址公园建设，推动开行"百年京张"主题旅游专列。

活化利用历史遗存，带动文化遗产保护传承。加强文物保护利用。将京张地区文物保护与老城保护、城市更新相结合，加强文物展示利用和活化利用，加快推进太子城考古遗址公园等建设，推出观光、研学、文化溯源旅游产品。提高非物质文化遗产保护传承水平。深入挖掘京张地区非物质文化遗产资源，推动非遗进社区，建设非遗特色村镇、街区和传承体验中心。提升工业遗产利用水平。强化工业遗产活化利用，推进旧厂区更新改造，加快推进新首钢高端产业综合服务区建设；鼓励利用工业遗产建设工业遗址公园、工业博物馆，打造工业文化产业园区、特色街区；打造以工业遗产为载体的体验式旅游、研学旅游等精品线路，改造利用老厂区、老厂房、老设施发展文化创意园区。

依托文化设施和文化服务，推动区域文化创新发展。繁荣文化艺术创作。支持开展以奥运会、长城国家文化公园等为主题的艺术创作，挖掘整理、复排提升一批传统（保留）剧目，创新推出一批旅游演艺精品，支持创作一批原创动漫精品，持续推动京张体育文化旅游带各艺术门类均衡发展。提升公共文化服务水平。推动图书馆、文化馆在奥运场馆等开设分馆，鼓励博物馆、美术馆、文化馆等建立合作联盟，创新开展主题文化活动和传统民俗文化活动。提升文化产业发展质量。加快发展数字创意、沉浸式体验等新业态，扩大数字文化产品供给，合理布局一批文化产业园区，打造协同创新发展平台。提高创意产品开发水平。大力推动奥运、长城、京张铁路等主题文化创意产品开发，加快培育具有京张地区特色文化元素的文化创意产品和旅游商品，促进创意设计与实体经济、现代生产生活融合发展。

● 世园公园首届冰雪嘉年华欢乐多

百年京张铁路遗址公园

　　1905 年，由詹天佑担任总工程师的京张铁路始建，并于 4 年后通车，这是中国人自主勘察、设计、施工和运营的第一条国有干线铁路，集中展示了中华民族近代工业文化精神，是国家和民族重要的文化遗产。这条铁路不仅拉近了张家口与北京的时空距离，同时演绎了一代代人、车、生活的精彩故事。百余年来，京张铁路与北京、张家口共同发展，它已经融入了百姓的生活记忆，并以其变迁承载起城市的记忆。

　　2019 年京张高铁通车后，老京张铁路停用。但这并不意味着京张铁路告别了历史舞台。通过创新改造，百年京张将以京张铁路遗址公园的形态继续陪伴北京城。通过加强对京张铁路清华园站、清河站、青龙桥站、康庄站、张家口站、宣化站等科学保护与创新利用，对詹天佑纪念馆进行改造提升，经过合理的拆除和保留后，京张铁路遗址公园将成为一座集遗址、文体、商业于一体，纵贯南北、横连东西的新型铁路遗址公园。

● 京张铁路遗址公园

三、推进区域旅游业高质量发展

京张体育文化旅游带内旅游资源丰富，北京冬奥会的举办极大地带动了区域体育旅游、冰雪旅游、文化体验和休闲旅游，有力推动大众旅游发展，为区域旅游产业发展注入新活力。未来，京张两地将进一步整合旅游资源，打造旅游精品，推进特色旅游，加强要素支撑，着力推进文体旅融合发展，推动区域旅游业发展再上新台阶。

打造区域精品旅游度假区，塑造国际旅游品牌。加强高等级旅游景区建设。推动景区与城区一体化发展，丰富产品、创新业态、提升服务，充分利用世界文化遗产，创建国家高等级旅游景区和世界级旅游景区。鼓励发展旅游

● 2022年7月24日，市民在北京世园公园露营文化节中体验皮划艇

● 2022年第13届北京奥运城市体育文化节在昌平举行

度假区。依托冬奥、冰雪、长城、世园、温泉、草原等资源，大力发展休闲度假旅游，提高旅游度假区的主题化、特色化水平，支持打造世界级旅游度假区。加强旅游休闲街区建设。积极发展文化体验、购物消费、演艺娱乐、特色美食等产品，推动打造一批文化特色鲜明的旅游休闲街区。推动乡村旅游提质升级。打造一批生态和民俗特色项目，推出一批全国乡村旅游重点村镇，优化乡村旅游产品供给。推进全域旅游发展。支持延庆区、昌平区推动全域旅游向纵深发展，支持崇礼区等旅游资源富集的区县发展以特色资源驱动全域旅游的产业模式。

发展区域特色旅游，丰富旅游产品供给。大力发展冰雪旅游。推动建设健身休闲、竞赛表演、运动培训、文化体验一体化的滑雪旅游度假地，推出一批冰雪旅游主题精品线路，建设一批冰雪旅游基地。大力发展自驾旅游。重点培育一批自驾游和露营地连锁品牌企业，打造生态、游憩、体验、运动等复合功能的自驾旅游交通路网，形成网络化的自驾车旅居车旅游服务体系。积极发展避暑旅游。推出山地自行车、山地越野、露营、徒步、野外拓展、滑草等系列产品，加强高品质避暑旅游产品开发和供给，引导以冰雪旅游为主的旅游景区和度假区探索发展夏季服务业态，大力推进"避暑＋研学旅游""避暑＋休闲度假"发展。

推进区域"＋旅游"融合发展，培育消费新热点。积极促进业态融合。推动体育、文化、旅游、科技、会展等多业态融合发展，开发一批以"冰雪体育休闲＋冰雪体育文化"为主题的户外休闲运动产品，积极打造体育＋旅游、非遗＋旅游、研学＋旅游等"＋旅游"产品，鼓励体育、文化、旅游与数字经济深度融合。培育消费新热点。支持开发集运动休闲、文化创意、康养度假等主题于一体的体育文化旅游消费新产品，打造夜间文化和旅游消费集聚区，鼓励开发一批以滑雪、骑行、露营等为代表的户外项目，积极培育定制消费、体验消费、智能消费、时尚消费等消费新热点。着力推进市场融合。鼓励体育、文化、旅游机构和企业对接合作，为体育文化旅游领域中小微企业、民营企业营造良好的发展环境，鼓励社会资本投资京张地区体育文化旅游项目。

● 张家口太子城小镇风光

● 张家口市宣化区为中小学生设立暑期专区体验5G科技的魅力

##　斯巴达勇士赛

　　始于 2005 年的斯巴达勇士赛，是全球顶级障碍赛跑，每年在全球 42 个国家及地区举办 250 多场比赛，吸引了超过 1000 万人的参与。为了迎合更多参与者需要，斯巴达勇士赛还设置了团队赛、儿童赛等分支赛事。

　　作为一项新兴赛事，因其充满野性的赛事理念、酷炫的赛程设计以及优质的参赛体验，斯巴达勇士赛在业内已经积累了相当高的人气。该赛事自 2016 年进入中国，目前已经举办了 61 场比赛。举办地从北上广深等一线城市，逐渐蔓延覆盖全国各地区，共计吸引超过 22 万人次的参与，线上线下观赛人数超过 15 亿人次。

　　2020 年，斯巴达勇士赛首次落地张家口崇礼，为期 3 天的比赛，共吸引了近万人次参与。为保障参赛者和爱好者的需求，比赛期间加开了数列北京至崇礼的高铁。同时，由崇礼滑雪小镇为选手们提供了全面的餐饮、住宿、医疗等保障。

● 2022年8月6日，斯巴达勇士儿童赛在北京世园公园拉开帷幕

四、深入推进区域协同发展

北京冬奥会的筹办带动京张两地交通设施相连相通、生态环境联防联治、产业发展互补互促、公共服务共建共享，区域协同发展成效显著。赛后，将以京张体育文化旅游带为抓手，深化区域协同发展，进一步构建区域快旅慢游交通体系、共建区域优美生态环境、促进区域产业分工协作、完善区域公共服务，努力推动京津冀协同发展取得新成效。

依托陆路和航空交通网络，构建区域快旅慢游交通体系。以京张高铁、京礼高速等干道为主骨架，依托北京首都、大兴机场和张家口宁远机场航空网络，围绕京张两地各综

● 中关村延庆园体育科技创新园

合客运枢纽、旅游集散中心、自驾车营地、旅游休闲驿站、奥运场馆、滑雪场、重点旅游景区度假区、特色村镇等重要节点，创新"高铁＋域内旅游公交"等新型旅游交通模式，打造空地立体、连通区域、沟通城乡、串联各类节点、衔接快慢的区域快旅慢游交通体系。运用 5G、大数据、人工智能、区块链等新一代信息技术，加速推进新型智慧交通基础设施建设，搭建交通能源互联网，推行移动、无感、智能交通安检技术，持续提升游客出行体验和出行效率。

推进产业分工协作，促进区域产业融合创新。推进体育运动装备研发制造。构建"北京研发定制＋张家口生产销售"产业链条模式，建设集装备研发、设计、制造、检测、

● 崇礼华侨冰雪博物馆

流通、仓储于一体的国家冰雪装备生产基地；依托张家口
高新区冰雪运动装备产业园、宣化冰雪产业园，研发雪服、
雪板等轻装备以及索道、造雪机等重装备，打造国家冰雪
装备生产基地。发展应用大数据及无人机产业。在共享数
据资源等方面强化大数据技术和思维的运用，加强无人机
产品在体育文化旅游领域的应用。共建产业创新平台。共

建体育科技和文化创意研发制造高地，加强中关村科技园区、中关村延庆园体育科技创新园、新首钢高端产业综合服务区等创新平台建设。

京张区域快旅慢游交通体系

航空： 2021年，首都机场共51家航司执飞航班，通航点175个，实现国内主要核心干线机场全覆盖；大兴机场共13家国内航司运营客运航线，开通国内航线146条，覆盖国内航点136个；张家口宁远机场共5家航司运营航线，执飞航线9条，通航上海、杭州、深圳、广州等11城。旅客也可先抵达首都机场或大兴机场，经北京轨道交通换乘至北京北站、清河站，乘京张高铁至张家口。

高铁： 京张高铁开通运营后，北京清河站至延庆站只需26分钟，北京清河站至张家口太子城站最快仅需50分钟。除京张高铁外，内蒙古、陕西、山西的游客可乘坐张呼、大西高铁、张大高铁高铁直达张家口，其他各省旅客可通过京沪高铁、京广高铁、京福高铁、京哈高铁到达北京后由京张高铁至张家口。

● 京张高铁

第六章　深入开展奥林匹克教育
持续推动社会文明进步

北京冬奥会的筹办和举办，有力地带动了全国2.5亿中小学生奥林匹克教育和校园冰雪运动的广泛开展，促进了青少年的健康成长和全面发展，全国共评选出835所奥林匹克教育示范校和2063所冰雪运动特色学校。全社会志愿服务精神进一步弘扬，带动更多人参与到社会志愿服务中来，进一步推动了中国志愿服务事业的发展，"志愿北京"信息平台实名注册志愿者人数达到443.6万人。全社会关爱、帮助残疾人，支持残疾人事业发展成为共识，主办城市无障碍环境显著提升，使残疾人更好地融入社会生活，包容性社会建设取得积极成效。冬季全民健身运动广泛开展，"经常参加体育锻炼"和"低碳出行"成为公众的生活方式，全社会文明程度显著提升，形成了宝贵的社会遗产。冬奥会后，将传承利用好这些宝贵财富，持续弘扬奥林匹克精神，深入开展奥林匹克教育，传播志愿服务精神，推动包容性社会建设，促进各项社会事业的繁荣发展，进一步增强全社会的幸福感和获得感。

一、深耕奥林匹克教育

冬奥筹办带动青少年奥林匹克教育取得丰硕成果，形成了具有中国特色的奥林匹克教育遗产。冬奥会后，将持续深入开展青少年奥林匹克教育，促进奥林匹克运动和奥林匹克精神在校园体育教育中的发展，普及冰雪运动，推动中小学生掌握冬季运动技能，广泛开展国际交流，培养青少年国际视野和文明礼仪风尚，深化奥林匹克教育特色示范学校、冰雪运动特色学校、同心结学校遴选，发挥示范作用，形成形式多样的教育教学模式，推动奥林匹克教

● 专注匠心——孩子们用非遗面花做冬奥会吉祥物

育向纵深发展，进一步提升中小学生综合素质，促进青少年全面发展。

深入推动奥林匹克教育教学。全国中小学继续将奥林匹克教育纳入学校教育教学内容，通过综合实践活动课程、体育课程、德育活动等方式，开展奥林匹克主题教育。推动冰雪类专项运动技能学习进入义务教育"体育与健康"课程，健全校园冰雪运动教学、训练、竞赛和管理体系，进一步加强学校冰雪运动场地设施和师资队伍建设，推动政府主导、部门协作、社会参与的校园冰雪运动推进机制更加成熟。在国家中小学智慧教育平台开设"冬奥精神冠军说""冬奥精神师生说""冬奥精神志愿者说"和"走进冬奥冬残奥"等栏目，面向广大中小学生讲好冬奥故事、传播冬奥声音，弘扬北京冬奥精神。

扩大奥林匹克教育示范成果。继续做好奥林匹克教育示范学校和青少年校园冰雪体育传统项目特色学校、试点县（区）、改革试验区的创建和遴选工作，充分发挥示范引领作用，吸引和带动全国中小学校积极参与，推动全国中小学校园冰雪运动特色学校到2025年达到5000所。建设好"北京国际奥林匹克学院"等研究机构，持续推出高质量奥林匹克运动研究成果，打造国际奥林匹克教育和人才培养的重要平台。2022年世界奥林匹克日，首都体育学院（北京国际奥林匹克学院）与希腊国际奥林匹克学院签署合作备忘录，双方将发挥各自优势，在奥林匹克教育、基础建设、师生互访、科研合作、奥林匹克文化推广等方面进行合作交流。

广泛开展奥林匹克教育文化活动。持续组织开展冬季奥林匹克知识普及和文化艺术活动，继续举办奥林匹克教育大课堂、冬季奥林匹克教育周、教育日、主题班会、冬令营等多种形式的主题教育活动，以冬奥文化为元素，继续组织开展中小学生音乐节、合唱节、舞蹈节、戏剧节等艺术活动和征文、绘画、摄影、知识竞赛等文化活动。持续推动"共赢未来"中外青少年人文交流活动和"同心结"学校建设工程，扩大与各国家、地区"姊妹校"的结对范围，深入推进中外青少年国际文化交流活动，增进相互理解与友谊。

● 北京玉泉小学开启"冰墩墩文化节"

二、传播志愿精神

北京冬奥会志愿服务工作卓有成效，为赛事成功举办发挥巨大作用，1.8 万赛会志愿者和 20 万人次的城市志愿者克服新冠疫情、冰天雪地、两地办赛等种种困难与挑战，用青春和奉献提供了暖心的服务，向世界展示了蓬勃向上的中国青年形象。北京冬奥会带动越来越多的人参与到社会志愿服务中来，截至 2022 年 10 月 18 日，全国实名志愿者注册人数达 2.29 亿，志愿服务队伍达 132 万个，累计服务时长近 51.6 亿小时。冬奥会后，将传承和利用好北京冬奥会志愿服务人才遗产和宝贵经验，进一步带动全社会弘扬冬奥志愿精神，培育文明风尚，健全志愿服务体系，壮大志愿服务队伍，推动我国志愿服务事业持续健康发展。

健全志愿服务制度。推动志愿服务制度化建设，打造多部门参与、联动高效的协调机制。规范志愿者招募注册制度，根据群众实际需要发布招募信息，根据标准和条件吸纳社区居民参与志愿服务活动，依托各级志愿服务信息平台组织登记注册。推动志愿服务标准化建设，优化志愿服务评估体系。加强志愿者服务立法工作，健全志愿服务法律体系，强化志愿者权益保障。加强志愿者培训管理，开展志愿者知识与技能培训，提高服务能力和服务水平，注重在实践中培养服务意识。健全志愿服务激励机制，完善志愿服务积分兑换、星级认定等回馈激励制度，规范志

● 2022年服贸会上志愿者在进行志愿服务

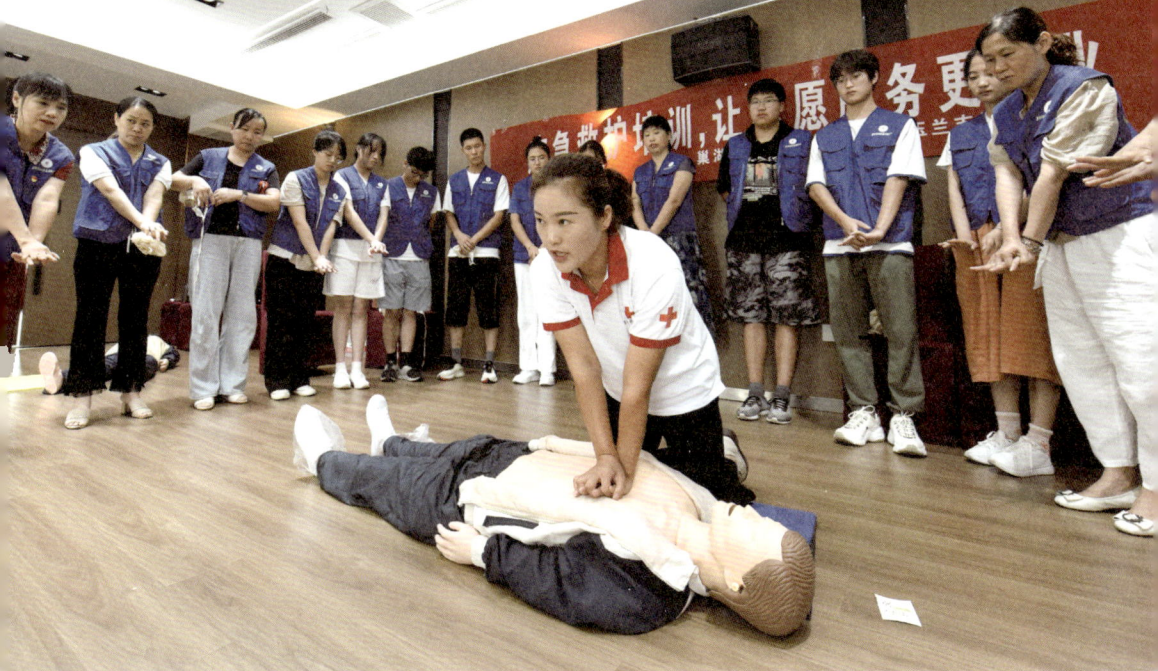

● 志愿者在进行医疗培训

愿服务记录与证明。

拓宽志愿服务平台。积极构建多元志愿服务平台，推动政府部门和社会力量共同参与。加大志愿服务组织培育力度，完善组织体系，鼓励有条件的地区建立专门的志愿服务组织孵化基地，建设一批活动规范有序、作用发挥明显、社会影响力强的示范性志愿服务组织，壮大志愿服务队伍。积极搭建志愿服务活动平台，不断拓宽志愿服务领域，扩大志愿服务覆盖面。利用好各类公共服务设施，根据实际需要建设志愿服务站点。立足需求、着眼民生，搭建志愿者、服务对象和服务项目供需对接平台，切实使服务对象受益。加大科技支撑，提升志愿服务信息化水平，探索"互联网＋

志愿服务"模式，创新服务方式。建设志愿服务宣传平台，传播志愿精神，弘扬志愿服务文化，讲好新时代志愿故事。北京冬奥会志愿者招募平台系统，赛后将保留沿用，并优化提升功能，为未来北京市大型活动志愿者工作搭建可靠高效的网络平台。

开展多种形式的志愿服务活动。推进公共事业的志愿服务，发挥志愿服务成本低、效率高的特点，积极支持志愿服务组织承接扶贫、济困、扶老、救孤、助残、救灾、助医、助学等领域的志愿服务。组建志愿服务队伍，建立对口联系、定向帮扶机制，扎根基层、服务群众，提升城乡文明程度。大力开展扶贫济困志愿服务活动，以生活困难群众、老年人和残疾人为重点对象，开展送温暖、献爱心志愿服务活动，为群众排忧解难。推动大型社会活动志愿服务，借鉴北京两届奥运会志愿服务的成功经验，组织好重大活动、重要会议和大型文体赛事的志愿服务。积极开展应急救援志愿服务活动，动员志愿者广泛普及防火避险、疏散安置、急救技能等应急处置知识，积极参与重大自然灾害和突发事件的抢险救援、卫生防疫、群众安置和心理安抚等工作，提升社会和公民应急处置能力。冬奥会后，北京和张家口两地的856个冬奥城市志愿服务站点也将根据城市功能规划和市民需要适当保留，服务于未来的城市志愿服务活动。

三、推动包容性社会建设

北京冬残奥会的筹办和举办，极大地带动了全社会助残扶残意识的提升，关爱、尊重残疾人的社会氛围更加浓厚。

● 中国志愿服务网

通过广泛开展残疾人冰雪活动，吸引更多残疾人参与冬季健身，体验冰雪运动的快乐；主办城市无障碍环境建设和服务水平显著提升，使越来越多的残疾人走出家门，出行更加方便；通过基层社区为广大残疾人提供康复护理、职业技能培训和法律维权等服务，使残疾人更好地融入社会。截至 2021 年 12 月，北京市创建 666 家温馨家园，年受益残疾人 391.4 万人次；张家口市分别有 7.5 万和 5.5 万名残疾人享受了生活补贴和护理补贴。未来，将管理和运用北京冬残奥会遗产成果，在残疾人关爱服务、无障碍设施完善、包容性社会建设等方面持续加大力度，为残疾人创造更高水平的无障碍环境和便利生活条件，使残疾人能够更加平等地参与社会生活。

传承推广冬奥无障碍设施建设标准。为满足冬残奥会办赛需求创新编制的《北京 2022 年冬奥会和冬残奥会无障碍指南》《北京 2022 年冬奥会和冬残奥会无障碍指南技术指标图册》等技术规范，全面提升了主办城市无障碍环境建设标准，推动《北京市无障碍环境建设条例》修订和出台。赛后，将持续完善和提升无障碍环境建设标准和规范，加强新（改、扩）建工程无障碍审查，建立无障碍环境定期评估制度，有序推进无障碍环境改造，新（改、扩）设施严格执行无障碍相关标准规范。同时，传承利用好《北京2022年冬奥会和冬残奥会无障碍中国方案》中的经验与成果，为未来我国体育赛事和活动的无障碍环境建设、管理和运行提供可借鉴、可推广的宝贵经验，更好地促进中国无障碍环境建设与发展。

全面提升无障碍环境建设水平。北京冬残奥会后，冬奥场馆和赛区的无障碍设施将保留并持续沿用，同时将进一步推动城市无障碍环境的改善和提升，在城市更新、

● 《北京2022年冬奥会和冬残奥会无障碍中国方案》摘录

● 河北省张家口市宣化区温馨家园残疾人展示亲手制作的冬残奥会主题手工艺品

乡村振兴、城市慢行系统建设、老旧小区改造、智慧城市建设等城乡建设和公共服务项目中统筹推进无障碍建设。从城市道路、公共交通、社区服务设施、公共服务设施和残疾人服务设施、残疾人集中就业单位等方面加快开展无障碍设施建设和改造；推广应用信息无障碍标准，加快政府政务、公共服务、电子商务、电子导航等信息无障碍建设；加强数字化服务线下引导和支撑，提供更多易操作的智能化服务，着力解决残疾人在运用智能技术方面的困难；探索建立无障碍设施认证体系，推动无障碍设施标准化和规范化建设。

持续推动包容性社会建设。继续营造全社会助残扶残的文明社会氛围，丰富残疾人精神文化生活。健全残疾人关爱服务体系，提升残疾人康复、教育、文化、体育等公共服务质量，推进残疾人充分就业，激发残疾人自强不息精神，鼓励残疾人自尊、自信、自强、自立，鼓励残疾人通过生产劳动过上更好更有尊严的生活。北京市未来将进一步推动街（乡）普遍建立服务残疾人的温馨家园，持续开展职业康复劳动、心理健康、法律维权、志愿助残等综合服务，增强基层为残疾人服务的能力。继续办好全国助残日、国际残疾人日和"残疾人事业好新闻评选"等主题宣传活动，加强无障碍知识和理念宣传教育，增进"首善有爱、环境无碍"的社会共识。

"

残疾人制作北京冬残奥会颁奖花束

北京冬残奥会颁奖使用的花束是采用中华传统非物质文化遗产独特工艺"海派绒线编结技艺"制成的绒线花。其制作是由北京脊髓损伤者希望之家召集北京市 10 个区 150 余位残疾人及其家属费时 2 个多月完成的。500 余束冬残奥会颁奖花束，包括 79474 片花瓣、12560 片叶子，共计 638 万多针，平均每束花耗时 35—40 小时，累计共耗时 2 万多小时。

● 北京冬奥会和冬残奥会颁奖花束

第七章

传承利用冬奥文化遗产
为美好未来注入生机活力

北京冬奥会既是一场体育盛会，更是一次新时代中国文化的集中亮相和展示，让全世界感受了中华文明的独特魅力和生机活力，用"中国式浪漫"完美诠释了奥林匹克精神，为奥林匹克文化打上了深深的中国印记，为现代奥林匹克运动可持续发展贡献了中国智慧。七年筹办，在冬奥文化设施、文化活动、文化产品和文化传播方面创造了丰厚的文化遗产，带动了"中国设计"和"中国制造"，推动了奥林匹克文化和冰雪文化在中国的传播；七年筹办，凝聚了全国各族人民的万众一心、勇毅前行的昂扬激情，孕育了伟大的北京冬奥精神；七年筹办，促进了世界多元文化与中华优秀传统文化的交流互鉴，增进了世界各国人民的友谊，发出了"一起向未来"的时代强音。冬奥会后，将弘扬北京冬奥精神，传承利用好冬奥文化遗产，促进体育文化事业发展，加强国际体育文化交流，进一步丰富世界奥林匹克文化，推动中华文化的创新发展，为人民幸福生活注入精神力量，增强国家文化软实力，共促世界文明进步的美好未来。

一、传承与弘扬北京冬奥精神

伟大事业孕育伟大精神。在北京冬奥会申办、筹办和举办过程中，广大冬奥建设者、工作者、志愿者、参与者不负使命、牢记重托、奉献担当、奋力拼搏，共同创造了胸怀大局、自信开放、迎难而上、追求卓越、共创未来的"北京冬奥精神"，凝结了北京冬奥会的精神成果，形成了北京冬奥会最重要的文化遗产和精神财富。北京冬奥会后，将持续传承和发扬北京冬奥精神，激励广大人民群众奋发向上、接续奋斗，把北京冬奥精神转化为全面建设社会主义现代化国家、实现中华民族伟大复兴的精神动力。

——胸怀大局：心系祖国、志存高远，把筹办、举办北京冬奥会、冬残奥会作为"国之大者"，以为国争光为己任，以为国建功为光荣，勇于承担使命责任，为了祖国和人民团结一心、奋力拼搏。

——自信开放：雍容大度、开放包容，坚持中国特色社会主义道路自信、理论自信、制度自信、文化自信，以创造性转化、创新性发展传递深厚文化底蕴，以大道至简彰显悠久文明理念，以热情好客展现中国人民的真诚友善，以文明交流促进世界各国人民相互理解和友谊。

——迎难而上：苦干实干、坚韧不拔，保持知重负重、直面挑战的昂扬斗志，百折不挠克服困难、战胜风险，为了胜利勇往直前。

——追求卓越：执着专注、一丝不苟，坚持最高标准、最严要求，精心规划设计，精心雕琢打磨，精心磨合演练，不断突破和创造奇迹。

——共创未来：协同联动、紧密携手，坚持"一起向未来"和"更团结"相呼应，面朝中国发展未来，面向人类发展未来，向世界发出携手构建人类命运共同体的热情呼唤。

弘扬北京冬奥精神。立足新起点、迈向新征程，必须继续传承和弘扬北京冬奥精神，转化为全面建设社会主义现代化国家的精神力量。弘扬北京冬奥精神，要激发广大人民群众"胸怀大局"的使命担当和爱国情怀，汇聚民族复兴的精神动力；要促进改革开放、增进团结友谊，传递"自信开放"、相互尊重、包容发展的精神内涵；

胸怀大局
自信开放
迎难而上
追求卓越
共创未来

联合主办
北京奥运城市发展促进会　中共北京市朝阳区委员会

北京冬奥精神

● 北京冬奥精神展在奥林匹克塔举办

要践行奋力拼搏的中华体育精神，激发"迎难而上"的大无畏民族气概和顽强斗志；要激励不断创新、勇于突破、精益求精的精神追求，发扬"追求卓越"的干事创业精神；要传递中国人民与世界人民携手共进、守望相助、"共创未来"的美好期待，向世界发出携手构建人类命运共同体的热情呼唤。

二、挖掘与利用北京冬奥文化遗产

北京冬奥会筹办和举办期间，形式多样、内容丰富的冬奥文化设计、文化活动、文化产品等传播了奥林匹克文化和冰雪文化，充分展示了长城文化、春节文化、非遗文化等中国优秀传统文化的独特魅力，为奥林匹克运动发展增添了新的文化动力。赛后，将深入挖掘冬奥文化遗产和资源，利用好冬奥文化设施，增添城市新型文化空间，丰富公共文化设施网络，持续举办冬奥和冰雪主题的文化活动，丰富公共文化服务供给，以冬奥元素为带动繁荣文化创意产业发展，不断满足广大人民群众日益增长的精神文化需求。

持续利用好冬奥文化设施。赛后将传承利用好冬奥文化广场、冬奥社区、三赛区奥林匹克公园等公共文化设施，

● 太子城遗址公园

推进城乡公共文化服务体系一体建设，创新培育城市公共文化空间，形成优质均衡、便捷高效的公共文化设施网络。利用冬奥文体设施，积极开发锻炼健身、休憩娱乐、展览展示功能，增加普惠性公共文化服务功能。妥善安置冬奥公共文化景观，鼓励将其移入公园、广场、博物馆等，长期向市民展出，保留冬奥记忆，丰富城市文化。继续推进北京奥运博物馆和北京国际奥林匹克学院建设，打造国际交往中心功能建设的独特窗口，高品质运营清华大学奥林匹克艺术研究中心、崇礼华侨冰雪博物馆、张家口太子城遗址公园等冬奥文化教育设施，搭建奥林匹克文化、艺术、研究的交流平台。

● 2022年8月5日全国大众欢乐冰雪周在呼和浩特开启

● 艺术家用15个不同的"冬"字灵动演绎出了北京冬奥会的15个运动项目

　　持续举办冬奥主题文化活动。赛后将继续组织举办好群众性冰雪文化活动，健全活动机制，拓展群众参与度。持续开拓全国大众冰雪季、全国大众欢乐冰雪周、北京市民欢乐冰雪季等群众性品牌冰雪文化活动，持续办好国际奥林匹克日等奥运文化活动，持续推广中国冰雪大篷车、冰雪知识微课堂等冬奥与冰雪文化知识传播活动，筑牢冰雪运动群众基础，促进冰雪文化融入百姓生活。继续鼓励冰雕、雪雕、冰蹴球、冰嬉、冰上舞蹈、雪地赛马、古老皮毛滑雪等各地传统冰雪文化的深入挖掘、保护、展演和推广，展示中国"冰雪故事"，丰富百姓文化体验。积极发掘冬奥文化资源，广泛开展各类冬奥文化艺术作品展览展示、交流研讨，文化艺术创作，冰雪影视、音乐作品展演传播活动，让冬奥文化艺术普惠百姓，持续传播奥林匹克精神和中华体育精神。

繁荣冬奥主题文化艺术创作。广泛开展群众文艺创作和活动，继续扶持以奥运、冰雪文化、长城文化为主题的音乐、影视、戏剧、电视节目、动漫等文化艺术创作。用好国家艺术基金、首都影视精品创作生产扶持项目、中国艺术节、各大剧院服务平台等，进一步完善全链条扶持机制。鼓励公共文化机构与社会力量围绕文化授权、创意设计、生产加工、营销管理等产业链深度合作。传承冬奥文创经验，注重文化内涵挖掘，提升科技含量，创新营销方式，完善企业、市场与院校协作的文创产、学、研体系。北京和张家口将大力推动奥运、长城、京张铁路等主题文化创意产品开发，提升"京张好礼"的吸引力与品牌影响力。

❝

千余枚冬奥徽章在北京奥林匹克森林公园展出

　　在北京冬奥会期间，"双奥之城的魅力——奥林匹克徽章上的北京故事"奥林匹克徽章展在北京冬奥会主新闻中心展出，使全球的媒体记者近距离感受北京的城市文化。冬奥会结束后，近千枚徽章整体搬移至北京奥林匹克森林公园的"廉洁奥运"主题展馆内长期展出，免费向市民开放。"小徽章，大文化"，记载了"双奥之城"北京多年的升华和蜕变，让观众在参观的同时领略到奥林匹克精神与北京悠久历史文化的独特魅力。

● 奥林匹克徽章展

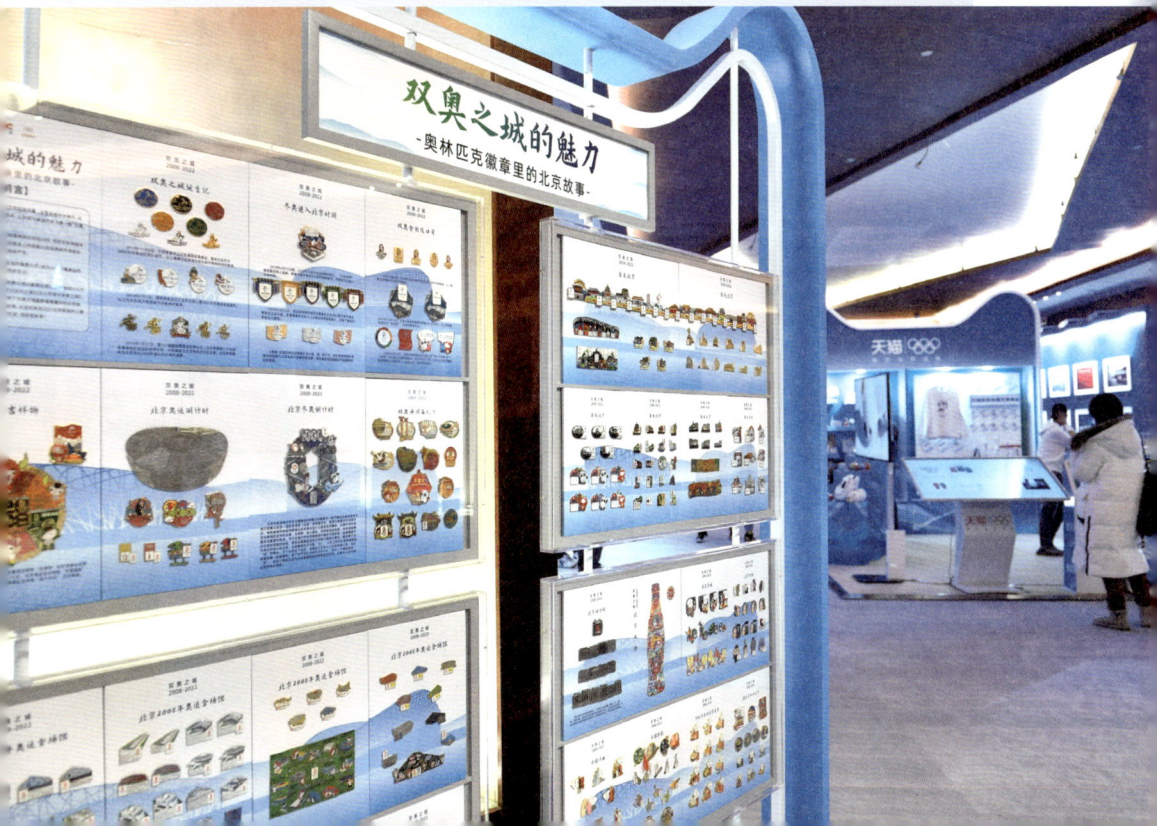

北京奥运城市发展促进中心

北京奥运城市发展促进中心作为北京 2008 年奥运会和北京 2022 年冬奥会的"双奥"遗产机构，将面向未来，大力弘扬奥林匹克精神，践行"传承奥运，促进发展"的宗旨和"创新发展，和谐共赢"的工作理念，为促进奥林匹克运动的可持续发展，为深入实施全民健身国家战略、加快推进体育强国建设和健康中国建设做出积极贡献。

北京奥运城市发展促进中心将按照"四个发展战略"确立的目标，加强顶层设计，创新体制机制，不断提升奥运遗产传承能力，推动"双奥"遗产传承事业高质量发展。

——充分发挥奥运遗产传承机构的职能作用。管理和利用好"双奥"遗产，举办北京奥运城市体育文化节、北京国际体育电影周、奥林匹克教育、"双奥"文化推广等活动，全力推进北京奥运博物馆建设，宣传奥林匹克运动，宣传北京，持续巩固传播奥林匹克精神传承奥运遗产的主阵地。

——充分发挥奥运遗产传承的国际交流作用。加强与国际奥委会、各国际单项体育组织、世界体育大会、世界奥林匹克城市联盟、奥林匹克博物馆联盟、米兰国际体育电影电视节等国际机构的交流合作，相互借鉴，相互合作，打造助力北京国际交往中心建设的独特窗口。

　　——充分发挥奥运遗产传承的共享借鉴作用。搭建有效平台，统筹双奥遗产共享，深入开展"双奥之城"实践经验和遗产成果梳理和总结，持续开展奥运遗产研究和成果转化工作，为双奥遗产传承奠定可持续发展的重要基础，建设输出大型赛事和大型活动经验的高端智库。

　　——充分发挥双奥遗产传承的辐射带动作用。整合软硬奥运遗产及体育文化旅游资源，加强城市及区域合作，积极为做好奥运场馆赛后利用献言献策，与延庆区、张家口市合力建设博物馆矩阵，推进奥运遗产项目共建联办，构筑促进京张体育文化旅游带建设的有效力量。

三、加强国际体育文化交流

北京冬奥的筹办向世界传递了中国同世界各国团结一致、"一起向未来"的强烈信号，始终保持与国际奥委会等国际体育组织的紧密良好关系，确保筹办工作符合奥运标准，积极服务国家（地区）奥委会和残奥委会，让各国运动员和贵宾充分感受中国人民的热情好客，推动实现173个国家共同签署奥林匹克休战决议，以体育交流拓展人文和经济交流，服务"一带一路"建设，使北京冬奥会真正成为对外开放的助推器。赛后，将持续发挥冬奥会的品牌效应，加强中外文化交流和多层次文明对话，深化与国际体育组织交流合作，进一步开拓与冰雪强国、友好城市、奥运城市的国际交往，推动民间文化合作交流，推动国际

● 2022年9月北京奥运城市发展论坛在首钢三高炉举行

"百城千屏" 推广活动

自"百城千屏"超高清视频落地推广活动（以下简称"百城千屏"活动）启动以来，全国多个地区先行先试、积极响应，一大批超高清户外大屏和8K电视率先在北京冬奥会前完成部署，圆满完成"百城千屏8K看奥运"赛事直播活动。经过北京冬奥会8K直播的实践，"百城千屏"活动成为受到广大人民群众广泛认可的新生事物。"百城千屏"活动将有效满足全国各地市民收看超高清节目、体验新视听科技的需求，拓展市民的新视听公共服务空间，共同享受冬奥会带来的科技进步成果。

● 北京市民通过8K显示屏在街头观看冬奥会闭幕式

体育文化交流迈上新台阶。

深化与国际组织的交往。赛后将持续加强与国际奥委会、国际残奥委会和国际单项体育组织的合作，引进和打造一批有特色、效果好、影响力大的国际顶级赛事。继续巩固和保持与各友好城市、国家（地区）奥委会之间的沟通联络，持续开展训练交流、友谊比赛和文化探访等相关文体交往活动。探索与冰雪强国和奥运城市开展体育交流新途径，扩大和深化冰雪运动项目、冰雪运动产业、冰雪文化领域的国际交流合作，带动我国冰雪运动的可持续发展。以"双奥之城"品牌影响力为依托，北京市将积极吸引国际体育组织、国际冰雪机构、职业体育联盟、冰雪运

● 青少年在2022年服贸会体育板块体验滑雪机

● "北京友好城市青年营"在京召开

动国际知名企业落户，扩大冬季运动项目推广，拓展中国冰雪市场，助力北京国际交往中心功能建设。

拓展多领域国际合作。传承利用北京冬奥会的国际交往经验，持续提升"欢乐春节""相约北京"国际艺术节等品牌活动的国际影响力。发挥我国历史文化资源优势，以历史文化资源和文化产业为依托，开发符合国外受众需求的文化和旅游产品，打造对外交流品牌。推动各地发挥地缘、人缘优势，加强城市间文化和旅游交流合作，持续推动文化产业国际合作。通过承接和举办各类国际组织年会、国际会展、国际会议等形式，推动经济、文化、旅游、教育等领域的务实合作。提高数字科技赋能，大力推广"云交往"等线上国际交往模式。

开展丰富多样的民间交流。发挥企事业单位、民间团体、社会组织的各自优势，广泛开展国际文化体育交流活动。加强同我国驻外机构和友好合作机构的沟通合作。发挥海外华文学校语言教学推广和文化传播作用，挖掘侨团侨社、行业协会、地区同乡会、文艺文化剧社的文化传播潜力等。依托奥林匹克社区、特色街道社区，探索街道社区层面的民间国际交流。向海外推广中国优秀民俗冰雪项目，利用世界奥运城市联盟等国际平台，加强与奥运城市间的国际交往，打造民间对外交往新亮点。

一起向未来

Together for a Shared Future

Prologue

The Olympic and Paralympic Winter Games Beijing 2022 (Beijing 2022) were an iconic event of great historical importance in China. After seven years of tough preparation, under the strong leadership of the Chinese Government and in close collaboration with the International Olympic Committee (IOC), International Paralympic Committee (IPC) and International Winter Sports Federations (IFs), the Chinese people have overcome many difficulties and challenges, and successfully presented a "streamlined, safe and splendid" Olympic Winter Games to the world in a "green, inclusive, open and clean" manner.

The success of Beijing 2022 was a fulfillment of the solemn promise made to the international community. Beijing has since then become the world's first "host city for both summer and winter editions of the Olympic Games" and has once again made the history of the Olympic Movement and shared the Olympic glory with the world.

Beijing 2022 was not only a spectacular sports gala, it has also created and left behind a wealth of Olympic legacies. The ambitious goal of "engaging 300 million people in winter sports" has been achieved. People across the country, especially the youth, have been greatly inspired to take part in winter sports, thus opening a new era for global winter sports.

The preparations for Beijing 2022 have strongly propelled the further development of the areas in and around Beijing and Zhangjiakou, and promoted the regional coordinated development in transport infrastructure, environment protection, industrial growth and public services.

Shougang area has become a new landmark of urban revival; Yanqing is building itself into "a unique tourist hub" and Zhangjiakou is developing into an international winter tourism destination.

The public has enjoyed rich benefits arising from Games preparation. The development of the ice and snow industry has facilitated local poverty alleviation, brought a dramatic increase in employment and improved living conditions.

Accessibility has been significantly improved in the host city and the services for people with disabilities have been rapidly developing. The spirit of voluntary service has become widespread and civility has improved across the society.

Those remarkable legacies and achievements have been detailed in the Legacy Report of Beijing 2022 (pre-Games) released by the Beijing Organising Committee for the 2022 Olympic and Paralympic Winter Games (Beijing 2022

Organising Committee) in 2021.

This edition is a post-Games legacy report, which focuses on the post-Games plans and key measures through leveraging the Beijing 2022 legacy to continuously promote the winter sports, the development of the city and region, and the social progress.

The report comprises 7 chapters, including winter sports popularisation, post-Games use of Olympic venues, ice and snow industry growth, host city development, building of Beijing-Zhangjiakou Sports, Cultural and Tourism Belt, and cultural and social developments.

Contents

CHAPTER 3

OPTIMISATION OF ICE AND SNOW INDUSTRY TO BUILD A MODERNISED INDUSTRIAL SYSTEM

CHAPTER 4

BEIJING 2022 PROMOTING HIGH-QUALITY URBAN DEVELOPMENT

CHAPTER 5

EXPEDITING THE DEVELOPMENT OF "BEIJING-ZHANGJIAKOU SPORTS, CULTURAL AND TOURISM BELT"

Chapter 1

CONTINUOUS POPULARISATION OF WINTER SPORTS TO PROMOTE THE DEVELOPMENT OF FITNESS-FOR-ALL PROGRAMME

The preparation for and staging of the Olympic and Paralympic Winter Games Beijing 2022 (Beijing 2022) propelled the rapid development of winter sports in China. A total of 346 million people have participated in winter sports across the country since 2015, and the vision of "engaging 300 million people in winter sports" has become reality. This is the greatest legacy that Beijing 2022 has created for the global development of winter sports and the Olympic Movement. It has significantly grown the global population participating in winter sports, thus providing more room for the development of ice and snow industry around the world.

The success of Beijing 2022 is not the end, as the popularisation of winter sports and the development of Fitness-For-All Programme is a long-term national strategy, which is a powerful means to promote the building of a healthy China. China will provide continuous policy support for the popularisation and development of winter sports. The country will organise more public winter sports activities and build more quality winter sports venues and facilities. Furthermore, the training of winter sports athletes will be strengthened and the competitive level of winter sports elevated, in order to bring China's winter sports to new heights.

Continuously Promoting Winter Sports for All

Beijing 2022 has ignited the people's enthusiasm for winter sports, which are booming with unprecedented vitality and momentum across the country. However, compared with China's population, winter sports still have great development potential in the country. China will continue to promote ice and snow culture and host a variety of public winter sports events that cater to different groups of people and younger generations.

Increase the efforts to publicise winter sports. Winter sports knowledge is being strongly promoted and popularised in China.

- To encourage the public to follow, enjoy and take part in winter sports. Promotional videos, animations and songs will be produced and winter sports readers. Handbooks, fitness guides and sports training pamphlets will be compiled and distributed.

- To expand the communication channels for the ice and snow culture. Information and media platforms, such as television, radio, newspapers and magazines, are encouraged to run winter sports programmes and columns.

- Ice and snow events will be widely organised online to step up the publicity of ice and snow culture, winter sports knowledge and winter sports events.

Continue to stage mass winter sports events.

- Well-received national mass winter sports events, such as the National Public Ice and Snow Season, will continue to play their leading role in engaging more people in winter sports, with a view to further expanding the population and geographical coverage of winter sports.

• National mass winter sports events in non-snow seasons, such as the National Public Joyful Ice and Snow Week, will continue to take place to break the seasonal restrictions and extend the time span of winter sports.

• Relying on local natural and cultural resources, popular winter sports events in diverse forms and with distinctive features will continue to be staged for the public across the country.

• The National Winter Sports Festival for People with Disabilities will continue to be held, and more winter sports events and competitions suitable for them will also be staged. Para sports will be promoted, the Paralympic concepts will be further spread, and better conditions for people with disabilities to engage in winter sports will be created.

Improve the standards to regulate mass winter sports. The formulation of national and local technical standards and regulations will be reinforced for the standardised development of winter sports.

• Develop the sport grading standards and approaches for mass winter sports, so as to unify the assessment work and improve the overall skill level of the participants in mass winter sports events.

• Develop the standards and guidelines for staging public winter sports events. In future, the holding of such events will comply with professional standards and service guidelines, so as to strongly guarantee the standardisation and regulation of such events.

Enhance the popularisation of winter sports among the youth. Winter sports programmes will be extensively carried out on campus, and the effort to establish Olympic Education Demonstration School and schools with winter sport programmes will continue across the country. Schools in southern China with necessary conditions are encouraged to provide more "simulated skating and skiing" classes to help the children shift from roller skating to ice skating. Schools with appropriate venues are encouraged to establish a competition calendar for winter sports meets or festivals and to promote the development of students' winter sports clubs.

To foster children and young people's interest in winter sports, events such as World Snow Day and International Children's Ski Festival, Youth Summer and Winter Camps and Youth Winter Sports Event Series will continue to take place. International communication and collaboration in youth winter sports will be further strengthened and more exchanges and communication events will be held with countries that are advanced in winter sports.

Building More Quality Winter Sports Venues and Facilities

Since the start of the preparation for Beijing 2022, winter sports venues and facilities in China have increased significantly. By early 2021, China built 654 ice rinks and 803 indoor and outdoor ski venues, a 317% and a 41% increase compared with 2015, providing a solid support for the popularisation and promotion of winter sports. In future, to provide more convenience for the public to participate in winter sports, China will make the following efforts:

- To find more existing venue resources that can be used for winter sports,

- To build more winter sports venues and facilities based on local conditions,

- To continuously improve the services and support provided for winter sports venues,

- To construct more winter sports venues for people with disabilities.

Find more existing venue resources for winter sports. In order to increase the availability of winter sports venues, further efforts will be made to use existing venue resources, encourage multiple use of venues and build more diversified ice rinks and ski fields. General winter sports centres will be created by upgrading the functions and facilities of existing sports venues. Existing ski venues will be supported to expand their capacity and improve their service standards. The way of rebuilding old factory workshops, warehouses and commercial facilities into indoor winter sports venues will also be recommended.

Build more winter sports venues and facilities based on local conditions. Using natural water resources, such as rivers and lakes, and open waters in parks to create natural ice rinks will be further encouraged. More ski venues will be built by relying on local natural resources, if the climate, topographical and ecological conditions permit.

Public sports venues, public squares with appropriate conditions will be encouraged to set up seasonal, temporary or removable winter sports venues for public recreation and entertainment events, and schools to build temporary ice rinks on squares and playgrounds to satisfy the demands of teaching and off-school activities.

The building of alternative winter sports facilities will be expedited, such as grounds for roller-skiing and roller skating, simulation ice rinks and removable ice rinks, in schools, parks, sports centres, tourism areas and shopping malls.

Build high-quality winter sports venues and facilities. The distribution of winter sports venues and facilities will be properly planned, and areas with suitable conditions will be encouraged to include venues for mass winter sports, such as public indoor and outdoor ice rinks and skiing venues, in their urban planning.

The "1,000 Ice Rinks in 100 Cities Programme" will continue, aiming to provide the public with mass winter sports venues that are affordable and convenient.

Promote the building of winter sports venues for people with disabilities. More winter sports venues and facilities will be supplied for people with disabilities. Accessibility renovation will be carried out for existing sports venues and sports equipment tailored to people with disabilities will be provided for those venues. Simulated winter sports fit for them will be developed and para winter sports coaching will be offered to them.

The venues of Beijing 2022 will actively support the development of winter sports for people with disabilities and the accessible facilities in these venues will remain available permanently.

Improve the service standards of winter sports venues. The public services at winter sports facilities will be further improved and increased, and the management will be regulated. Winter sports venues will be encouraged to open to the public for free or at low cost. Intelligent management systems will be adopted and venue information service platforms will be built to create user-friendly, smart and digital venues.

All-round Improvement of the Competitive Level of China's Winter Sports

Beijing 2022 has remarkably upgraded the competitive level of China's winter sports. To get the Chinese national team well prepared for the Games, China took multiple efforts, such as targeted development of winter sports, application of new technologies in training, and enhanced training of backup teams. As a result of these efforts, the Chinese national team successfully took part in the competitions of all the sports and achieved its best records at both the Olympic and Paralympic Winter Games. The outstanding performance of Chinese athletes and their impressive results have become the pride of the Chinese people and will surely inspire more people to participate in winter sports. In future, China will continue to focus on the all-round development of winter sports, the training of new athletes, and the elevation of its overall competitive level of winter sports.

Promote the all-round development of winter sports. In terms of the future development of winter sports, China will promote the balanced development of all winter sports by further improving its advanced sports, such as Short Track Speed Skating, stepping up the support for its underdeveloped sports, such as Ice Hockey, and planning and developing new sports, such as Nordic Combined.

In terms of geographical distribution, different areas will

target on the development of different winter sports according to the characteristics of sports and regional advantages. Heilongjiang, Jilin and Liaoning Provinces in Northeast China will be encouraged to develop more winter sports; the development of winter sports in North and Northwest China will be expedited, and other areas will be mobilised to develop the sports that suit them. Regional collaboration and resource sharing will be strengthened to promote the cross-region development of winter sports.

Improve the training of winter sports athletes. A diversified athletes training system will be in place with sports schools, colleges of physical education and professional sports teams as the main part and primary and middle schools and universities, enterprises and private sports organs as the supplement, with a view to establishing teams that feature all age groups, full sports programme and high-standard professional training.

The role of selecting athletes through competitions will be emphasised to find more promising athletes for the teams. The building of training bases for high-level athletes will be enhanced, and the training facilities and the team of trainers for athletes will also be improved.

Continue the development of competitive winter sports for people with disabilities. The Beijing 2022 Paralympic Winter Games have promoted the development of winter sports for people with disabilities across the country. Winter sports are becoming more popular among them and their competitive level is improving remarkably.

For the next step, further efforts will be made to build a training system for amateur athletes to expand the team of backup athletes, build sports training bases and provide training for more professional coaches, referees and classifiers. Top coaches will be recruited from abroad to provide training and outstanding athletes will be selected to join the national teams, with a view to winning more honours at future international sports events.

Fostering the Team of Winter Sports Workers

Promoted by the preparations for Beijing 2022, the number of winter sports professionals in China has kept on growing, thus laying a solid foundation for the popularisation and development of winter sports. By June 2022, the number of winter sports instructors reached 29,000 in Beijing. After Beijing 2022, China has continued all these efforts in order to provide a powerful workforce to support the sustainable development of winter sports in the future.

Enhance the training of winter sports instructors. Instructors for winter sports have been included in the national sports instructor system, and winter sports knowledge and skills training has been a part of the general training programme for all sports instructors. An examination and evaluation system for winter sports instructors will be established, aiming to upgrade overall professionalism and qualification of winter sports instructors.

Strengthen the training of various winter sports workers. The institutions of higher education are encouraged to adopt winter sports as one of their majors or curricula, and set up winter sports training bases and research centres to conduct targeted and professional training programmes. In response to the development of mass winter sports, training programmes will be offered to management, technical and skilled personnel engaged in winter sports event planning and organisation, ice and snow industry management, winter sports facility maintenance and management, and winter sports protection and rehabilitation. Meanwhile, various winter sports events will provide field training opportunities for personnel specialising in event organisation.

Diversify the training for winter sports personnel. The standardisation of the training system for winter sports personnel will be carried out; an evaluation mechanism based on skill assessment for winter sports personnel will be established; and the work of developing skill standards, organising training courses and issuing qualification certificates will be regulated. More support will be given to private training organisations, and diverse educational resources will be used for winter sports training. Professional technical training for the workers of mass winter sports will be held online and offline and advanced international professional training courses will be introduced to provide people involved in work of winter sports with diversified technical training and services.

Enhancing the Development of Social Winter Sports Organisations

Since 2015, social winter sports organisations in China have seen rapid development. They have played an active role in popularising winter sports and supporting winter sports enthusiasts. By December 2021, the number of officially registered winter sports organisations in China has reached 792, eight of which are national-level associations and 32 are provincial-level ones, representing a 2.8-fold increase compared with 2015.

As the public demand for winter sports keeps growing, China will continue to promote the development of social winter sports organisations, support the innovative development of the national winter sports federations and establish diversified sports clubs for mass winter sports, propelling the development of winter sports in the whole country.

Improve the structure of winter sports organisations. The structure of social sports organisations will be improved, establishing a system with the general sports federations at the top, the winter sports associations, industrial and mass sports associations as the pillars and various social sports organs at the grassroots level.

The winter sports organisations at each level will be encouraged to expand themselves and do their best in developing winter sports among the public from social sectors, creating more popular winter sports events and activities for the public.

Promote the innovative development of national winter sports associations. National winter sports associations will be gradually transformed into independent entities. Their functions, systems and roles in relation to mass sport and sports culture will be strengthened to amplify their public influence.

To date, the Chinese Skating Association, the Chinese Figure Skating Association and the Chinese Ice Hockey Association have become independent entities and are fully functional. Next, the Chinese Ski Association, Chinese Curling Association, Chinese Nordic Combined Association, Chinese Bobsleigh and Skeleton Association and Chinese Luge Association will do the same.

Build diversified mass winter sports clubs. Local winter sports associations are encouraged to expand their club and individual memberships and to give full play to the role of different types of mass winter sports organisations. These mass winter sports organisations will gradually group into networks in urban and rural areas.

The 8th Beijing Winter Sports Festival

Beijing Winter Sports Festival, created in 2014 and organised by Beijing Municipal Government, has taken place for eight consecutive years, with the last one held between December 2021 and April 2022. The online and offline events of the festival have drawn residents from across the city. To encourage more people to take part in the events, a total of 120,000 free tickets were given out to residents who won in an online quiz. A wealth of winter events were staged in 34 venues in 26 parks across the city, which saw a total of 1.4 million participants.

Furthermore, Beijing Radio and Television Station opened radio talk shows on two of its columns, namely "1025 Sports Life" and "101 Possibilities of Sport" to popularise the knowledge about the Olympic Winter Games and winter sports. A total of 198 talks were given, reaching over 59.4 million listeners. According to statistics, 9,075 winter sports activities were held at the festival, drawing a record of 16.9 million participants (not including listeners of the talk shows). As the winter sports event series held at the festival continue to gain popularity, the festival will play an even greater role in propelling the high-quality development of mass winter sports in Beijing.

Lucheng Fitness-For-All Centre in Tongzhou District of Beijing

The construction of Lucheng Fitness-For-All Centre in Beijing Municipal Sub-centre is expected to complete by the end of 2022. The Centre has four gyms with a total floor area of about 48,000 m², as well as an outdoor sports field of about 10,000 m², where the local residents may engage in sports such as basketball, tennis, football, martial arts, swimming and skating. The Centre can satisfy the needs of about 50,000 local residents living within a 3 km radius for fitness, recreation, culture and sports.

Standards Improved to Support the Development of Winter Sports in Heilongjiang

Heilongjiang Province published the Classification of Alpine Skiing Venues on 29 January 2022, which provides important local standards for winter sports venues and facilities.

The Classification of Alpine Skiing Venues is based on the national standards prescribed in the Conditions and Technical Requirements for the Opening of Sports Venues; Part VI: Skiing Venues. It divides alpine skiing venues into I, II and III Classes, according to the quantities of skier-transport carriers, basic service facilities, skiing gears, machinery and equipment, and service crew. The classification clearly defines what types and classes of skiing events can be held and what winter sports services should be provided at the venues. It also serves as a guide for skiing enthusiasts to choose the skiing venues and services that are fit for them. This document has provided standards for the venue construction and the provision of services at the alpine skiing venues in the province and even the whole country, as well as guidance and guarantee for the rapid and healthy development of the ice and snow industry.

Chinese Skating Association Introduced "Grassroots Plan"

To consolidate the foundation for the sport, the Chinese Skating Association (CSA) introduced the "Grassroots Plan" in January 2020. To date, the Plan has been progressing well. Based on the model of "club open competitions + boot camps + training" , which enjoys high public participation, the "Grassroots Plan" has been carried out to train skating coaches, instructors, learners and referees at grassroots level. The implementation of the Plan has ensured that systematic and scientific training is provided and has substantially elevated the training standard of grassroots clubs. It has expanded the reserve of athletes and laid a solid foundation for the sustainable development of the sport.

The Plan was started with the increase of clubs. The CSA plans to set up 1,000 skating clubs across China within five to seven years.

Based on this, top-level and branded club open skating competitions of the boot camps will be organised through the involvement of professional trainers. In terms of training, the boot camps will focus on the basic skills and new techniques, all-round physical development, mental-health education and counselling, nutritional and dietary advice, injury prevention and first-aid knowledge.

The "Grassroots Plan" aims to turn out top skating athletes for each province and municipality before the National Games of China in 2024 and the Olympic Winter Games in 2026 through five years of execution. Each of the participants in the Plan is expected to play a key role in the future development of skating.

Chapter 2

POST-GAMES USE OF
BEIJING 2022 VENUES

The post-Games use of Beijing 2022 venues was taken into full consideration in the early stage of venue planning and construction. The venues have not only satisfied the Games-time needs, but will also serve the future development of the host city. Among all the 12 competition venues, 4 were venues for Beijing 2008. In order to secure the post-Games use of venues in advance, the development of the Venue Legacy Plan of all the competition venues and main non-competition venues of Beijing 2022 was launched 4 years before the Games, which has become an effective tool to ensure the smooth transfer of the venues into legacy mode.

During the Games, these beautiful venues displayed to the world the perfect combination of the Chinese traditional culture and the Olympic elements, as well as the ingenious craftsmanship of the Chinese architecture. After the Games, all the venues will be open to the public and host world-class sports events throughout the year to support the sustainable development of the city and the region. All efforts will be made to ensure that the venues of Beijing 2022 will be in extensive and lasting use in the future, making them the invaluable and benefiting legacies from the Olympic Games.

Playing Host to Top-level Sports Events

During the preparation for and the staging of Beijing 2022, the venue owners established good relations with the NFs and the IFs. After the Games, they will continue their collaboration with the sports organisations at home and abroad to apply for and play host to premier international and national sports events, which will effectively promote the mass sports events, the national Fitness-For-All programme and local development.

Strengthen the collaboration with sports organisations at home and abroad. The communication and exchanges with IFs and NFs will be increased. In addition to staging local, national and international sports events, the venues will do their best to provide services for the training programmes of the Chinese national teams, professional sports teams, youth and individuals, as well as the academic exchange activities related to sports medicine and sports science, for instance:

National Aquatics Centre. The World Curling Federation and the Chinese Curling Association have reached an agreement to set up a World Curling Academy Training Centre;

National Speed Skating Oval. The venue will become home to the International Skating Union Centre of Excellence (CoE). As the first CoE in the world, it will promote and popularise skating in China and around the world;

National Sliding Centre and the International Bobsleigh and Skeleton Federation (IBSF) have signed a memorandum of understanding and agreed to regularly host IBSF calendar events and training camps at the centre.

Apply for and stage international sports events. To increase their popularity at home and abroad, these venues have endeavored to bid for and stage top international winter sports events, such as World Cups, World Championships, Intercontinental Cups, Asian Cups and Tournaments. They take the international sports events as a wonderful platform to promote the positive interaction between sports events and commercial activities.

Big Air Shougang, the first permanent big-air venue in the world, will apply for the hosting of the FIS Freestyle Skiing and Snowboard World Cups.

National Alpine Skiing Centre is also bidding for the hosting of such events as the FIS Alpine Ski World Cup.

Play host to national winter sports events. Working closely with the Winter Sports Management Centre of the General Administration of Sport of China and the National Winter Sports Associations, the venues of Beijing 2022 will play host to various national and regional winter sports events, such as the National Winter Games of China, national tournaments, championships, youth winter sports meets and youth U-series league competitions. The events will promote the development of winter sports events and activities in the surrounding areas.

In the future, National Speed Skating Oval will stage various national ice sport events, including speed skating, short-track speed skating, figure skating, curling and ice hockey.

National Indoor Stadium will be the venue for the ice sports events of the Beijing Youth Championships and the 2nd Beijing Winter Games.

Opening Olympic Venues to the Public

Staging sports events and serving public fitness activities are essential for the post-Games use of the Olympic venues. To date, all the competition venues of Beijing 2022 have finished the transition from Games-time to post-Games use. They are fully open to the public and have organised a wealth of events, such as Olympic winter sports experiencing, public fitness practice, sports demonstrations, venue tours and exhibitions.

In the future, following further renovation and improvement, the venues will be able to provide more diverse and interesting events to better meet the public needs for different fitness and recreational activities. These venues will provide constant support for the development of the national Fitness-For-All programme.

Adaptation of venue facilities to cater to public use. To provide better services for the public, some of the venues have made necessary adaptations to make the facilities suitable for the public to carry out fitness-related activities. While maintaining the capability to host professional sports events, they will organise easy and engaging activities for the public. The transition from exclusive use by professional athletes to inclusive use by general public has expanded the user groups of the venues and raised the rate of venue utilisation.

Genting Snow Park: the ski tracks for halfpipe, slopestyle, parallel and cross competitions are now also open to the public after adaptations to reduce the technical difficulty.

National Sliding Centre: a starting point was reserved for the public on the north side of the 380-degree spiral curve during its construction, which reduces the vertical drop of the track from 121 metres to over 40 metres and allows the public to safely enjoy "the fast and the furious" on ice.

Opening of venues to the public. Opening the venues to the public is the most effective approach for social benefits. After Beijing 2022, based on their functions, the venues have planned relevant winter sports experience events and organised mass public fitness activities. These venues reproduced the scenes of the Games to organise venue tours for the visitors to cater for the public interest in the Games, and meanwhile, different Olympic winter sports experience events, training courses, recreational and fitness activities and mass sports events were organised in the venues to satisfy public demand for fitness.

National Aquatics Centre. It has been open to the public since April 16, 2022, with an event themed "Join Me in Curling—Experience Olympic Winter Sports Culture at the Ice Cube" taking place there on the same day. The venue received over 3,000 visitors on the first day of its opening, thus it was called humorously "the hottest ice" in Beijing.

Hold events for the public. The Beijing 2022 venues have been actively holding welfare and benefit events to offer the public free and low-cost opportunities for participation and kindle their consumption. More and more venues have taken part in the free-admission programme and they are also encouraged to open to the public with low admission fees in some time slots.

To help young people learn knowledge of Olympic winter sports and Olympic culture, the venues are working with educational institutions to provide open classes to the youth. Experience programmes designed for winter sports lovers of all levels have been offered, where professional coaches provide technical guidance and intensive training. These activities have further enhanced the enthusiasm of the public for winter sports.

Capital Indoor Stadium. It officially launched the "Public Winter Sports Benefit Programme", which called on the winter sports venues across China to "open to the public free of charge at least once a month", and to regularly offer to the public free winter sports courses that are interesting and easy-to-learn. The programme aims to make winter sports accessible to the public and the youth. A total of 33 winter-sports venues in Beijing, Tianjin and Hebei have become the first group to take part in the programme.

Promoting Year-round Venue Operation

After Beijing 2022, all the Games venues will be transformed into multi-purpose complexes, which will operate with different business formats throughout the year. Ice sports venues, most of which are indoor ones, will be open to the public all year round and stage various major sports events and cultural and recreational activities. Snow sports venues will be used for skiing events in winter and for outdoor sports, tourism and recreation and mountain holiday activities for the rest of the year, to achieve year-round operation.

Develop ice and snow sports. In order to promote winter sports consistently, various ice and snow events, including competitions and public winter fitness activities, will take place in Olympic venues throughout the year.

With an ice surface of 12,000 m^2, the National Speed Skating Oval has the capacity to accommodate over 2,000 people taking part in public experience activities or competitions in speed skating, short track speed skating, figure skating, ice hockey and curling simultaneously. Currently, 6,000 m^2 of ice surface are open to the public. Visitors may rent skates to experience speed skating on "the fastest ice", or have fun in various ice recreational and entertainment activities. On its first day of opening, the venue received nearly 1,000 visitors.

Develop sports in all seasons. Most of the Beijing 2022 ice-sports venues are fit for both summer and winter sports events and public fitness activities. After necessary renovations, they are able to operate all year round. Due to weather restrictions, snow-sports venues in Yanqing and Zhangjiakou will host snow sports competitions and experience events in winter. For the rest of the year, they will develop outdoor and mountain sports activities, such as jogging, cross country running, mountain cycling, mountaineering and rock climbing, hiking and grass skiing, and set up outdoor training centres as well.

National Cross-Country Skiing Centre will create a mountain and outdoor sports park that combines mountaineering, mountain cycling, trekking and rock climbing in the near future.

Develop diverse business formats. In addition to running different sports activities, each venue will make full use of local cultural, historical, and natural resources to develop different forms of commercial activities, such as regional tourism and recreational and mountain holidays, promoting the integrated development of sport, culture and tourism.

Big Air Shougang. Well known for its landscape lighting, the venue will focus on the staging of industrial-heritage styled commercial events, such as outdoor music fests, auto shows, concerts, beer festivals and light shows.

Genting Snow Park. The income of the venue from non-snow seasons already accounts for 90% of its annual revenue. Its featured family-recreational events include stargazing, children's summer camps and family music and art festivals.

National Ski Jumping Centre. The venue makes good use of its start and finish areas to hold conferences, football matches and concerts. Working with the conference and exhibition centre in Taizicheng Ice and Snow Town, the venue will play host to mountain and outdoor sports exhibitions and conferences.

Integrating into the Overall Regional Development

Upholding the concept of combining venue planning and construction with urban development plans, the venues of Beijing 2022 have supported the city's strategic positioning and promoted the development of sports and ice and snow industries. Moreover, they showcase the city's cultural elements and provide all-season tourist destinations.

Venues in Beijing Zone enhance the image of the "Olympic City". The venues in Beijing Competition Zone will provide strong support for Beijing's strategic development. Through the staging of various popular sports events, they contribute to the development of sports and Fitness-For-All programme in China and the promotion of cultural and sports communication among countries across the globe. Furthermore, they enhance the image of Beijing as the city ever to host both the summer and winter editions of the Olympic Games.

Phase II of China National Convention Centre. It will be the venue for staging events related to state and political affairs and top commercial exhibitions. Once opened, the entire convention centre will become a complex for conferences and exhibitions with a space of nearly 1.3 million m^2, making it "the city's reception centre".

Venues in Yanqing contribute to the building of "a unique

tourist hub in Beijing" . Yanqing Competition Zone serves the positioning of Yanqing District as an international sports and cultural tourism and recreational zone. As a key component of Yanqing's three major highlights, namely Beijing 2022, Expo 2019 and the Great Wall, the Yanqing Zone will play an important role in developing the all-year tourism in Yanqing.

Taking advantage of the Games facilities and cultural resources, Yanqing Zone is growing into the core area of ice and snow consumption in northern Beijing and an all-season holiday destination featuring fitness and outdoor activities, winter sports competitions, and mountain tourism.

The Yanqing Competition Zone formally opened to the public on 1 May 2022. It launched an Olympic site tourism programme, which allows tourists to have an Olympic venue sightseeing by taking the cable car to the start area of the National Alpine Skiing Centre, experiencing the sliding sports with simulation facilities at the National Sliding Centre, and staying at the Olympic Village to enjoy the same accommodation and food & beverage services for the athletes of Beijing 2022.

Olympic Venues in Zhangjiakou Zone contribute to the building of an international winter sports and tourism destination. The competition zone will support the city's vision to build a world-class winter sports, culture and tourism destination and its main goal of turning Chongli District into an international winter sports destination and a top conference and exhibition centre.

Relying on its existing tourism, cultural and sports venue resources, Zhangjiakou Zone is planning to introduce multiple business formats to the area, including sports events, exhibitions, performances, festivals, holidays, rehabilitation, health care, academic research and training, and promote in-depth integration of sports, culture and tourism.

Currently, the Zhangjiakou Chongli Olympic Park and Genting Snow Park are open to the public and some mass sports events, including Beijing-Zhangjiakou All-season Sports Tourism Carnival, have taken place there.

Chapter 3

OPTIMISATION OF ICE AND SNOW
INDUSTRY TO BUILD A MODERNISED
INDUSTRIAL SYSTEM

The popularisation of winter sports in China has strongly promoted the rapid development of the ice and snow industry. This has led to the initial formation of an industrial system composed of winter fitness and recreation, winter sports equipment manufacturing, ice and snow tourism, competitions and performances, sports training, venue services and ice and snow-themed conferences and exhibitions. The overall scale of China's ice and snow industry grew from RMB270 billion in 2015 to RMB600 billion in 2020.

After Beijing 2022, China will continue to upgrade and develop the ice and snow industry, further improve the industrial structure and expand its independent R&D capacity. The overall scale of China's ice and snow industry is expected to reach RMB1 trillion by 2025.

Winter Sports Equipment Manufacturing

Beijing 2022 has sped up the development of China's winter sports equipment manufacturing industry, with the variety of products, market scale and investment continuously increasing. By 2020, China had nearly 20 winter sports equipment industrial parks. In 2022, China's winter sports equipment industry is expected to generate over RMB20 billion in annual sales revenue, representing an average annual growth of over 20%.

After the Games, China will keep on promoting the development of winter sports equipment manufacturing industry, further expanding the supply capacity, producing internationally renowned local brands, and building more industrial parks.

Further optimise the industrial structure. To further implement the action plan for the development of winter sports equipment industry, the following actions will be taken in future:

- Strengthen the overall strategic planning for the industry;
- Continue to develop winter sports equipment manufacturing in Northeast and North China;
- Raise the R&D and manufacturing capacity of the sports industry clusters in the Yangtze River Delta, Pearl River Delta and regions west of the Taiwan Straits;
- Develop winter sports equipment for the public;
- Encourage the R&D of high-tech products;
- Build an integrated industrial chain for smart winter sports equipment.

Further step up the building of industrial bases for winter sports equipment manufacturing. The regions and areas with necessary conditions will be encouraged to establish industrial parks to bring together relevant enterprises and elevate their R&D, production and service capacities and form complete industry chains. For instance:

- Langfang in Hebei Province is speeding up the building of a leading ice and snow industry city. In addition to establishing industrial parks, the city has attracted major winter sports equipment manufacturers. It has expedited the development of a complete ice and snow industry chain which focuses on winter sports equipment manufacturing, R&D, ice and snow tourism, professional training and ice and snow culture.

- Jilin Winter Sports Equipment Industrial Park has drawn some major manufacturers in cable cars, snow cannons, carbon-fibre snowboards and ski outfits. The park has a planned investment of RMB300 million and occupies over 100,000 m^2.

Continuously enhance the independent R&D capacity of manufacturers. Guided by the vision of staging a high-tech Olympic Winter Games, China has been promoting industrial upgrade through technological innovations.

- The domestic winter sports enterprises will further enhance their R&D capacity to develop new brands of products and rise their market shares.

- Equal importance has been given to the introduction of advanced technology from abroad and the domestic R&D of products to raise the proportion of China-made high-end products.

- The allocation and sharing of research resources will be optimised for research institutions, universities and enterprises.

Ice and Snow Tourism

Beijing 2022 has propelled the rapid growth of ice and snow tourism, which has become quite popular among the public. Tourists and industrial revenue have seen remarkable increases; tourism enterprises and financial investment continued to grow; ice and snow holiday resorts mushroomed and ice and snow tourism market boomed. The number of tourists in China during the 2020 – 2021 snow season reached 230 million and the revenue amounted to RMB390 billion.

Ice and snow tourism is critical to promoting domestic consumption. After Beijing 2022, we will make good use of the Games legacy to continuously promote the development of ice and snow tourism, building more high-quality ice & snow holiday resorts and ski resorts.

Increase the supply of ice and snow tourism products. Relying on the rich venue resource of Beijing 2022, boutique ice and snow tourism products, winter sports events and training bases will be created. Yanqing District in Beijing and Chongli District in Zhangjiakou will be turned into world-renowned ski-holiday destinations and national sports-tourism demonstration areas. Furthermore,

- Province-level ice and snow holiday resorts and ice and snow tours with convenient transport, well-developed infrastructure, unique ice and snow sceneries will be provided across China.

• Commercial winter sports competitions and performances will be promoted to expand the winter sports market.

• Efforts will be made to develop ice and snow tourism in the rural areas, such as building ice and snow towns and villages.

Beijing will provide strong support for the building of Beijing Olympic Winter Park in the new Shougang area in the west part of the city. The park will feature new types of industrial tourism and a sports industry model zone which integrates professional sports competitions, fashion sports and high-quality tourism services. Meanwhile, Beijing will also turn the Beijing Olympic Green in the north into a hub of cultural, tourism, sports and conference and exhibition industries.

Expand the potential of ice and snow tourism demand. Popular ice and snow tourism products will be developed for both the domestic and international markets. Promotion and publicity of winter sports and ice and snow culture will be stepped up to inspire more people to participate. To stimulate the ice and snow tourism consumption and expand local market demands, some winter sports facilities will be transformed into ice and snow tourism complexes that combine culture, commercial and entertainment elements. Events of local-flavoured "Ice and Snow Day" will be encouraged across the country to attract more people to ice and snow tourism.

Hebei Province held the 2nd Beijing-Zhangjiakou All-season Tourism Carnival in July 2022. Focusing on sports tourism, the event greatly enhanced the recognition and influence of the Beijing-Zhangjiakou Sports, Cultural and Tourism Belt.

Promote the development of "ice and snow tourism +". To promote the development of ice and snow tourism + culture, the Beijing 2022 cultural legacies and local cultural resources will be well used to add more cultural elements to tourism events and festivities. Events like "ice and snow tourism + culture seasons" will be held.

To promote the development of ice and snow tourism+ education, the Beijing 2022 venues will work with schools to allow more young people to engage in winter sports by organising various activities such as study tours and winter camps.

To promote the development of ice and snow tourism + technology, online ice and snow tourism will be actively developed and the technological innovations of the Games will be widely applied in developing the ice and snow tourism, such as big data, cloud computing, the Internet of Things, blockchain and 5G network, BeiDou Navigation Satellite System and virtual reality.

Winter Sports Event Industry

Beijing 2022 has boosted the development of winter sports event industry in China. Winter sports competitions and performances are gaining more and more popularity and becoming an important pillar of local economy. Since 2015, plenty of high-level international winter sports events have taken place in China, including speed skating, ice hockey, curling, snowboard and freestyle-skiing big air. Spectator sports, such as snowboard, figure skating and short track speed skating, have become the most popular sports for the public. Various national and international winter sports events for the youth are also thriving across the country, which indicates the bright future of the development of winter sports.

After the Games, the Olympic venues will play host to national and international, professional and amateur winter sports events and performances, continuing to contribute to the development of public fitness and competitive sports.

The construction of Beijing-Zhangjiakou Sports, Cultural and Tourism Belt will provide a platform for top international winter sports events taking place in Beijing, Tianjin and Hebei, which will constantly promote the growth of winter sports and regional economy.

Foster the market of domestic winter sports events and performances. General winter sports events, such as the National Winter Games, will continue to be held and diversified to include mass sports competitions and activities for public participation. Mass winter sports events will be encouraged across the country to guide and promote the development of mass winter sports in the local areas. To promote the development of winter sports market, the following efforts will be made:

- Events and activities involving winter sports skills will be held in non-snow seasons, such as roller skating, roller skiing and grass skiing.
- More high-level professional winter sports events will be promoted in China to attract sports enthusiasts from around the world.
- Professional winter sports will be encouraged and developed and professional league competitions will be held for sports such as ice hockey.
- Private sectors will be supported to stage spectator sports events, such as figure skating, ice hockey, curling, snowboard and short track speed skating.
- Commercial winter sports performances will be encouraged to expand the market in China.

Promote youth winter sports events. More winter sports events will be organised for the young people across China.

- The winter sports programme of the National Youth Games will be expanded to engage more youth athletes in the competitions.

- Additional U-series winter sports events will be organised and more schools with winter sports programmes will be established to attract more young people to winter sports.

- Colleges and universities will be encouraged to build teams of competitive winter sports, and organise youth-club leagues.

- Various social sectors will be mobilsed to offer training programmes for the youth to practise winter sports, such as running sports schools, clubs, boot camps and off-school sports centres.

At the 2021–2022 Beijing Youth Ice Hockey Club League, 1,224 matches were held, which involved 256 teams with nearly 3,600 players from 25 clubs. The scale of the event has remained at the top in Asia.

Chapter 4

BEIJING 2022 PROMOTING

HIGH-QUALITY URBAN DEVELOPMENT

Beijing 2022 has greatly promoted the urban renewal and upgrade of Beijing and Zhangjiakou, and enhanced the prominence and influence of the host city. People have become more enthusiastic about sports and fitness activities, and the Olympic spirit has rooted deeply in people's heart. The developments of Shougang, Yanqing and Zhangjiakou are typical examples showing how Beijing 2022 has promoted the local development and how the win-win result has been achieved for the Olympic Movement and the host city.

Beijing 2022 will continue to serve as a driving force in the effort to turn Shougang into Beijing's new landmark of urban revival, build Yanqing into "a unique tourist hub in Beijing" and transform Zhangjiakou into an international winter sports, cultural and tourism destination. The Olympic legacy will provide lasting benefits for the high-quality development of the host city and improvement of people's life.

Shougang-Beijing's New Landmark of Urban Revival

Beijing 2022 has provided a historic opportunity to transform Shougang Park into an iconic example of urban regeneration through the reuse of industrial heritage. To support Beijing 2022, a number of Olympic Winter Games facilities and venues were constructed in the park, including the headquarters for the Beijing 2022 Organising Committee, the training base for the national teams and the Big Air Shougang, as well as a national sports industry demonstration zone.

With an emphasis on ecological protection, a total of 540,000 m^2 old industrial space was reused for new development. The industrial renewal project of Shougang Park has won a grand prize at the 1st Beijing's Best Practices of Urban Renewal.

After the Games, Shougang Park will continue to explore the innovative approach of reusing industrial heritage, implement the New Shougang Three-year Action Plan, and enhance the operation of Beijing Olympic Winter Park, to further develop it into an industrial transformation and upgrade pilot zone in the west of Beijing.

Further develop sports+ industries. Beijing 2022 legacies will be managed professionally and internationally through marketing, so as to enlarge their potential benefits. More actions will be taken, such as:

- An extreme sports park will be built to promote extreme outdoor sports, such as roller skating and rock climbing.
- Big Air Shougang will work with the related international sports organisations to hold top-level international sports events and offer professional training programmes.
- The Park will open to the public to provide them with diverse fitness activities and tourism products.
- The four training venues for short track speed skating, figure skating, curling and ice hockey will continue to provide training services to professional sports teams and stage related

competitions.

- The exhibition hall of China International Fair for Trade in Services will also be leased for indoor basketball training during non-exhibition periods to support public fitness activities.

Vigorously develop "technology+ industries". In line with Beijing's strategy to create an international innovation centre, the spaces of Shougang Park will be used to create a hub for technological innovation.

- The emerging industries of artificial intelligence (AI), science fiction and metaverse, which are youth- and future-oriented and have a global perspective, will be developed in the Park.

- Scenarios applications related to artificial intelligence will be carried out in the Park, such as smart driving.

- The ZGC Science Fiction Industry Innovation Centre, China Science Fiction Research Centre and related upstream and downstream enterprises will be invited to settle in the Park.

Create a park ideal for living and working. Adjacent to the new Shougang area that has been developed, two additional areas will be constructed to support industrial development.

One is the Jinzhou City Innovation Plaza, which will be built next to the existing Shougang area in west Beijing and focus on passing on the industrial culture, being people-oriented, and embodying the new concepts of smaller street blocks and dense road network, three-dimensional ped & bike system and open public spaces.

The International Talent Community will be an inclusive space. Capitalising on its downtown location, the community will attract top international talents and young entrepreneurs to create a multipurpose space that combines innovation and R&D, businesses and offices, sport and living, and quality leisure and recreation. This community will help reach the regional jobs-housing balance and achieve the sustainable regional development.

Yanqing–a Unique Tourist Hub in Beijing

Beijing 2022 has provided opportunities for Yanqing development. Infrastructure in the area has been upgraded, as the Yanqing section of Beijing-Chongli Expressway and Beijing-Zhangjiakou High-speed Railway have been opened to traffic in 2020. Sports and cultural tourism is developing rapidly, and over 100 high-quality homestay (bed and breakfast) hotels have been in service. The top three highlights of Yanqing, namely Beijing 2022, the Great Wall and Expo 2019, have boosted the recognition and influence of the city.

Yanqing will maximise the role of the Beijing 2022 legacies in further developing its ice and snow industry and all-year tourism, making continuous efforts to build "a unique tourist hub in Beijing"

Raise the city's international profile. Beijing 2022 has left Yanqing with some of the world-class venues and facilities, such as the National Alpine Skiing Centre and National Sliding Centre and the Yanqing Olympic Zone. Those tangible and intangible Olympic legacies are invaluable to the promotion of regional development. To maximise the role of Beijing 2022 legacies,

- Yanqing Competition Zone will continue to hold top-level national and international alpine skiing, bobsleigh and skeleton and luge competitions after the Games.

- All of the Beijing 2022 venues in Yanqing will open to the public, offering a variety of mass winter sports experience programmes and activities.

- More pubic ski facilities will be built in ski resorts to encourage skiers of all levels to take part in winter sports.

- In non-snow seasons, Yanqing will take full advantage of its cultural, historical and natural resources to develop mountain holidays, leisure tourism and outdoor sports to keep the venues operating around the year.

These efforts will help develop Yanqing Olympic Zone into an internationally popular holiday and ice and snow tourism destination.

Moreover, high-level cultural events including festivities, conferences and exhibitions will take place to widely advertise the highlights of Yanqing, fully integrating the legacies of Beijing 2022, Expo 2019 and the Great Wall in its drive to build "a unique tourist hub in Beijing".

Develop the ice and snow industry. Yanqing is a key component of the development of the "Beijing-Zhangjiakou Sports, Cultural and Tourism Belt". In the post-Games period,

- Yanqing will continue to popularise winter sports and build more public winter sports facilities.
- The Vanke Shijinglong Ski Resort will be expanded and a "snow-fun park" will be added to the Badaling Ski Resort.
- Relying on the teaching resources of the Beijing Institute for International Olympic Studies, Yanqing will set up China's first national experimental area for the programme of winter sports on campus, aiming to strengthen winter sports-related training and cultural communication.
- The building of Zhongguancun (Yanqing) Centre for Cutting-edge Sports-technology Innovation will be expedited.
- An ice and snow industry chain will be developed, which will fully integrate with tourism, education and science and technology.

Increase the added value of tourism industry. Thanks to Beijing 2022, Yanqing has become a well-known city, which thus boosted the growth of its tourism industry tremendously. As a model area for developing all-year tourism, Yanqing will further increase the added value of tourism industry chain by providing more and better services and products.

To this end, the industry of homestay inns (bed and breakfast) developed and soon flourished in Yanqing, and some of them have become famous brands, such as "Winter Sports Homestay", "Expo 2019 Homestay", "Great Wall Homestay" and "Mountain & River Homestay". The homestay industry has not only supported the ice and snow tourism, but also brought income to the local people. A total of 600 homestay inns will be built and 150 popular brands created by the end of 2025.

The local traditional cuisine streets will be upgraded to make Yanqing a popular food tourism destination. Tourist souvenirs peculiar to Yanqing will be developed and local produce, such as fruits and vegetables, meat and food grains, will be sold as tourist commodities under the brand of "Gui Shui Agriculture".

Zhangjiakou-an International Winter Sports and Tourism Destination

Beijing 2022 has brought about remarkable achievements in infrastructure construction, industrial transformation, eco-environment improvement, urban and rural facility upgrade and public welfare in Zhangjiakou, laying a solid foundation for fast and all-round development of the city.

In future, Zhangjiakou will prioritise the building of the Beijing-Zhangjiakou Sports, Cultural and Tourism Belt. To achieve the goal, Zhangjiakou will focus its efforts on the post-Games use of the Olympic venues, the full integration of culture and tourism, the development of ice and snow economy and the promotion of renewable energy.

Promote the post-Games use of Olympic venues. Beijing 2022 has left Zhangjiakou with a large number of competition and non-competition venues, including the Genting Snow Park, Guyangshu venue cluster, Zhangjiakou Olympic Village and Zhangjiakou Medals Plaza. Next, the Venue Legacy Plan will be effectively implemented and the infrastructure and supporting services will be improved. To turn Chongli into a world winter sports destination, the venue owners will work with the local authorities to develop the sectors of commerce, education, science and technology, culture, tourism and holiday in the surrounding areas. The ultimate goal of these efforts is to achieve the all-season operation of the Olympic venues and maximise the benefit from the Beijing 2022 legacies through developing the economic activities of sports competitions, conferences and exhibitions, forums and scientific researches.

Expand the ice and snow economy. Beijing 2022 provided

·

an opportunity for Zhangjiakou to develop the R&D and manufacturing of winter sports equipment upon its existing ice and snow resources and industries. The city has set up two ice and snow industrial parks, each occupying over 200 hectares, in its High-tech Industrial Development Zone and Xuanhua District. The capacity of the two parks will be further expanded and more enterprises will settle in the park to from a complete industrial chain. In the future, Zhangjiakou will be moving forward to a world-level base for winter sports and a hub for international ice and snow industries.

Promote integrated development of culture and tourism. Zhangjiakou boasts a wealth of cultural and tourism resources. The Beijing-Zhangjiakou High-speed Railway and the Beijing-Chongli Expressway now connect it to Beijing, a city with an enormous tourist market, allowing a large number of tourists to travel quickly to Zhangjiakou. After Beijing 2022, the city will upgrade its scenic areas and attractions and create cultural tourism products. Cross-region tourism and scenic area operation projects will be launched in Beijing and Zhangjiakou to further develop the all-year tourism. To date, 652 projects have been planned for future development of the "Beijing-Zhangjiakou Sports, Cultural and Tourism Belt", 46 of which have already been launched.

Develop a green industrial system. Beijing 2022 has

promoted the development of renewable energy + industries in Zhangjiakou, including the industries of photovoltaics, wind power, hydrogen and big data. A regional green-power trade mechanism has been established and a system comprising green-power transmission, storage and consumption formed.

In the future, efforts will be focused on the development of integrated storage of photovoltaic energy and wind power in conjunction with the building of a renewable energy model zone. The key projects of hydrogen industrial innovation centres and high-density hydrogen storage strategic industrial base will be expedited to make Zhangjiakou a national pilot hydrogen-industry city and hydrogen-power production bases. Zhangjiakou is also striving to develop itself into a centre of digital economy. As a part of the national "transferring computing power from east to west" project, a cluster of national data centres will be built in Zhangjiakou. Thus, the overall level of the local digital economy will see a tremendous elevation.

Top Three Tourist Itineraries in Zhangjiakou

Passionate Winter Sports Tour. It connects scenic areas and tourist attractions, including:

◆ Chongli venue cluster (including the National Ski Jumping Centre),

◆ Ski resorts,

◆ Zhangbei Sainadu Snow World,

◆ Kulun Nao'er Tourist Resort in Guyuan County, and

◆ Yuanyang Lake Ski Resort in Shangyi County.

More scenic areas and tourist attractions in this area will be added to the tour, such as:

◆ Chicheng Haituo Valley Holiday Resort,

◆ Chicheng Hot Spring Resort,

◆ Luanhe Shenyun Scenic Area in Guyuan County,

◆ Gushui Fuyuan Holiday Resort,

◆ Desheng Folk Culture Village in Zhangbei,

◆ Yehuling Military Fortress, Daqing Mountain Scenic Area in Shangyi County, and

◆ Shisanhao Village.

Historical and Cultural Tour. It primarily includes the following scenic areas and tourist attractions.

◆ Jiming Posthouse in Huailai County,

◆ Huanglong Mountain Villa,

◆ Mount Jiming in Xiahuayuan District,

◆ Xuanhua Ancient Town,

◆ Dajing Gate in Qiaoxi District, and

◆ Zhangjiakou Fortress and Youwei Fortress in Wanquan Town.

Ecological and Cultural-study Tour. It primarily includes scenic areas and tourist attractions, such as:

◆ Huailai World Wine Park,

◆ Guanting Reservoir National Wetland Park,

◆ Huailai Wine Estate,

◆ Dingling Memorial Hall,

◆ Remains of Yellow Emperor City in Zhuolu County,

◆ Nuanquan Ancient Town in Yu County,

◆ Yuzhou Museum,

◆ Little Mount Wutai and Jinhekou Scenic Area,

◆ Nihe Bay National Relics Park in Yangyuan County, and

◆ Sanggan River Gorge in Xuanhua District.

Chapter 5

EXPEDITING THE DEVELOPMENT OF "BEIJING-ZHANGJIAKOU SPORTS, CULTURAL AND TOURISM BELT"

Beijing 2022 provided a powerful driving force for the development of the Beijing-Zhangjiakou Sports, Cultural and Tourism Belt. In developing the competition zones in Beijing, Yanqing and Zhangjiakou, which are located in the key areas of the Belt, emphasis was placed on the integration of local sports, tourism and cultural resources. The Beijing-Zhangjiakou High-speed Railway and the Beijing-Chongli Expressway were built to provide quick transport connections among these areas. Meanwhile, coordination and support were strengthened in the fields of eco-environment, industrial development and public services. In short, the preparation for and staging of Beijing 2022 have effectively propelled the integrated development of sports, culture and tourism in the regions, as well as the development of the Beijing-Zhangjiakou Sports, Cultural and Tourism Belt.

After the Games, to give full play to the Beijing-Zhangjiakou Sports, Cultural and Tourism Belt in the coordinated development of the Beijing-Tianjin-Hebei Region, the Central Government, Beijing Municipality and Hebei Province have formulated a series of plans and taken related actions continuously. The Beijing 2022 legacies will be fully used to strengthen regional development and promote the innovative and integrated development of the sports, cultural and tourism industries, adding new vitality to the coordinated development of the Beijing-Tianjin-Hebei Region.

Promoting Rapid Development of Sports in the Region

Promoted by Beijing 2022, winter sports have been developed and popularised in Beijing and Zhangjiakou. A group of world-class winter Olympic venues and winter sports facilities have been built and winter sports events are thriving, which have laid a solid foundation for sports development in the region. The development of the Beijing-Zhangjiakou Sports, Cultural and Tourism Belt will centre around the Olympic venues to create a hub for sports events, conferences and exhibitions and a centre for the Fitness-For-All programme, which will further boost the development of the sports industries in the region.

Organise more sports events to make full use of the Beijing 2022 venues. Beijing 2022 venues will further improve their event hosting capacity and level of services so as to turn themselves into key venues for top national and international winter sports events.

To speed up the development of a sophisticated training system and enhance the training of winter sports athletes, more winter sports training bases will be built, such as the National General Training Bases in Yanqing and Chongli. Furthermore, world-level training programmes will be introduced, high-level winter sports coaches and trainers will be recruited, and the collaboration with national and international sports institutions will be strengthened.

Taking advantage of the advanced Games venues and facilities in Beijing and Zhangjiakou, the conference and exhibition industry will be further expended and developed in the region.

Develop a public service system for the Fitness-For-All programme.

Promoting winter sports,

• Free sports events, such as winter sports experience games and joyful ice and snow seasons, will be held for the public;

• More youth winter sports projects will be launched and popularised;

• Policies supporting the development of winter sports will be improved; and

• More winter sports pilot areas will be established across the region.

Expanding all-season sports,

• All kinds of seasonal and short-term sports, cultural and entertainment events will be encouraged;

• Supports will be given to parks to expand their sports facilities; and

• Cities with appropriate conditions will be encouraged to build large and well-equipped sports parks.

Improving sports for all service,

• Beijing 2022 venues will further upgrade their services and expand their capacities for hosting sports, public fitness, culture and recreation, and public benefit activities;

• More popular, well-equipped and professionally managed general sports complexes will be bult; and

• National-level sports industrial bases will be in place in the region.

Support the coordinated development of regional sports industries. Beijing 2022 venues with suitable conditions are encouraged to set up Games exhibitions as windows to communicate Olympic culture. The development of Beijing Olympic Winter Park, Yanqing Olympic Zone and Zhangjiakou Chongli Olympic Park is being expedited, so is the building of the Beijing Institute for International Olympic Studies.

All of the Beijing 2022 venues will be transformed into multi-purpose facilities for sport, culture, tourism, recreation and entertainment. Low-carbon operations of Beijing 2022 venues will be promoted.

To promote the construction of smart venues, new technologies such as 5G networks, 8K ultra high-definition videos, VR and AR, cloud computing and AI will be adopted in venue operations.

The Beijing 2022 venues will play an active role in

promoting regional development. Serving as indispensable resources for the development of local tourism and recreational industries, the venue clusters in Yanqing and Chongli will serve local holiday tourism to provide high-quality sports, recreational and conference facilities.

Building Regional Cultural Development Centres of the New Era

Beijing 2022 has promoted the development of Olympic culture in China and introduced to the world China's traditional and urban cultures, especially the history and culture of the Beijing-Zhangjiakou Sports, Cultural and Tourism Belt. After the Games, the development of the Beijing-Zhangjiakou Sports, Cultural and Tourism Belt will continue to promote the integration of Olympic culture, Chinese traditional culture, ice and snow culture and the Great Wall culture, and create new cultural-exchange platforms and forge new paths for sports and cultural development.

Enhance the influence of the Olympic city. The cultural and tourism features of Beijing Olympic Green and Beijing Olympic Winter Park will be expanded. Communication and collaboration with previous host cities of the Olympic Winter Games will be strengthened, to enhance Beijing's international influence as a "host city for both summer and winter editions of the Olympic Games".

A National Great Wall Cultural Park will be built, with "the Olympic Games at the foot of the Great Wall" as an important component of the Park. The Badaling section, the Chongli section and the Dajingmen Gate in Zhangjiakou will be well protected as a whole, and the spiritual, cultural and landscape values of the Great Wall will be further exploited. The Olympic culture and Great Wall culture will be preserved and promoted together in the Park.

The "Centennial Beijing-Zhangjiakou Railway Culture" will be promoted. The historical and cultural heritage and resources located along the Beijing-Zhangjiakou Railway will be protected and exploited, including the historical relics, revolutionary history and industrial remains. Efforts are being made to expedite the construction of the Beijing-Zhangjiakou Railway Relic Park and the launch of a special tourist train with the theme of "Centennial Beijing-Zhangjiakou Railway".

Utilise and protect historical relics and cultural heritage. Urban renewal will be combined with the protection, exhibition and utilisation of historical relics and cultural heritage in Beijing and Zhangjiakou, such as the Taizicheng Archaeological Park. Tourism products featuring sightseeing, academic research and cultural heritage will be developed.

The standards for the preservation of intangible cultural

heritage will be improved. The intangible cultural heritage in Beijing and Zhangjiakou will be further explored. Activities related to intangible cultural heritage will be held in local communities. Villages, townships and neighbourhoods with intangible cultural heritage will be confirmed, where experience centres will be built for the public to visit.

Industrial legacies will also be re-used. Old industrial areas will be transformed or renovated and the building of multiple industries in new Shougang will be expedited. The transformation of industrial legacies into industrial relic parks and museums will be encouraged and zones or commercial streets featuring industrial culture will be established.

Tourist products, such as immersive and research tours of industrial legacies, will be developed. Cultural creation parks built on old factories and old industrial facilities are also an option for the transformation of old industrial legacies.

Cultural facilities and services to promote the development of regional culture. To promote cultural and artistic creations, cultural and artistic projects around the subjects of the Olympic Games and the National Great Wall Cultural Park will be encouraged. Traditional drama will be recovered, reproduced and reperformed, and new and fine tourism and art performance products will be created. The production of high-quality original animation movies will be supported. All efforts will be made to continuously promote the development of different types of art in the Beijing-Zhangjiakou Sports, Cultural and Tourism Belt.

Public cultural services will be improved. For instance, libraries and cultural centres will be encouraged to set up branches at Beijing 2022 venues; museums, art galleries and cultural centres are encouraged to work together in staging thematic cultural events and traditional folk culture events. The development of cultural industries will also be enhanced.

New business formats, such as digital creations and immersive experience, will develop on a fast track. The supply of digital cultural products will be increased and a group of cultural industrial parks will be built to provide platforms for coordinated innovation and development.

The development of creative cultural and tourism products, particularly those related to the Olympic Games, the Great Wall and Beijing-Zhangjiakou Railway will be vigorously promoted. The integrated development of creative design and the real economy and modern living will be promoted.

Promoting the High-quality Development of Regional Tourism

The Beijing-Zhangjiakou Sports, Cultural and Tourism Belt boasts rich tourism resources. The staging of Beijing 2022 has greatly boosted sports, ice and now, cultural and recreational tourism in the region and brought new vitality to the development of local tourism industry. Beijing and Zhangjiakou will further explore their tourism resources and create quality tourism products.

Develop premium and internationally recognised holiday resorts. The construction of national scenic areas will be stepped up and the development of scenic areas will be included in urban planning. Further efforts will be made to deliver diversified tourism products, innovative business formats and improved services. The world cultural heritage will play a leading role in the creation of world-level tourist areas.

The development of holiday resorts will be encouraged. Resources such as Beijing 2022, the Great Wall, Expo 2019, ice and snow, hot springs and grasslands will be used to build such resorts. Holiday tourism will be a business format to be vigorously promoted and the development of world-class holiday resorts will be supported.

Tourism and recreational streets and plazas will be built, where cultural and tourism experience activities and facilities for shopping, performance, entertainment and food specialties will be available. Rural tourism will be further promoted and ecological and folk culture tours will be provided. To do so, tourism villages and towns will be built and rural tourism products developed across the country. Areas with unique tourism resources, such as Yanqing and Changping in Beijing and Chongli in Zhangjiakou, will be encouraged to develop all-year tourism.

Develop regional tourism to diversify tourism products. The development of ice and snow tourism will be prioritised. Ski and holiday resorts that integrate fitness and recreation, competitions and performances, sports training and cultural experience will be built, and more ice and snow tours will be put on the market.

Self-drive tours will be promoted and chain enterprises managing self-dive tours and campsites are encouraged. Self-drive tourism road networks and service systems that combine services of sightseeing, accommodation, catering, shopping and sports will be created.

Summer vacation tourism will also be promoted, with products of mountain biking, cross-country running, camping, hiking, outward-bound training and grass skiing. Ice and snow tourism scenic areas and resorts will be encouraged to provide services for summer vacation tourism. The business formats of "summer holidays + study tours" and "summer holidays + recreation" will be actively promoted.

Promote the integrated development of "region + tourism" to boost new consumption trends. The integrated development of sports, culture, tourism, science and technology and conferences and exhibitions will be actively promoted. Outdoor recreational and sports products under the theme of "winter sports recreation + winter sports culture" will be created, tourism products featuring sports + tourism, intangible cultural heritage + tourism and study + tourism will be developed, and the integration of sports, cultural, tourism and digital economy will be encouraged.

New tourism products combining sports, recreation, cultural creation, health and holiday will be promoted to foster new consumption trends. Night cultural and tourism fairs and plazas and outdoor tourism products such as skiing, cycling and camping will be encouraged. New consumption trends will be created, including customised, experience-based, smart and fashion shopping.

Collaboration between sports, cultural and tourism agencies and enterprises is recommended and favourable environments will be created for micro, small and medium-sized and private enterprises to develop in the fields of sports, culture and tourism. Furthermore, social capital will be encouraged to invest in sports, cultural and tourism projects in Beijing and Zhangjiakou.

Promoting Coordinated Regional Development

The preparations for and staging of Beijing 2022 propelled the interconnection of transport, the joint ecological and environmental control and protection, the development of complementary industries, the co-development and sharing of public services in Beijing and Zhangjiakou.

After the Games, the development of Beijing-Zhangjiakou Sports, Cultural and Tourism Belt will be taken as the key to the coordinated development of the region, and a propeller for the construction of fast-travel and slow-visit transport system, the building of a beautiful ecological environment and the improvement of public services in the region.

Rail and aviation networks to help develop fast-travel and slow-visit transport systems for tourism. With the rapid transit infrastructure including Beijing-Zhangjiakou High-Speed Railway and Beijing-Chongli Expressway as well as Beijing Capital International Airport, Beijing Daxing International Airport and Zhangjiakou Ningyuan Airport as the main framework, a fast-travel and slow-visit transport system for tourism will be in place.

This transport system extends to local passenger-transport hubs, tourist centres, auto campsites, Olympic venues, ski resorts, main scenic spots, holiday resorts and rural villages and towns. The innovative tourism-transport model of high-speed railway + regional tourism buses combines air and land transport, connect urban and rural areas and reach out to all tourism destinations, allowing the tourists to spend less time on the way and more time on their visits.

The building of smart transport infrastructure will be expedited, in which the latest information technologies, including 5G, big data, AI and blockchains, will be used. A traffic-energy Internet will be developed and technologies for mobile and smart transport security checks will be adopted to effectively raise the travel efficiency and improve visitors' experience.

Promote the industrial division and collaboration between industries. An industrial chain in the form of research and development in Beijing + manufacturing and sale in Zhangjiakou will be established to form a national-level winter sports equipment manufacturing base, which combines functions of research, design, manufacturing, testing, distribution and storage. The national winter sport equipment manufacturing base will be built in Zhangjiakou, which is composed of the Winter Sports Equipment Industrial Park in

Gaoxin District and the Xuanhua Ice and Snow Industrial Park involved in the production of light equipment, like skis and skiwear, and heavy equipment and machinery, like cableways and snow guns.

Big-data and drone industries will be developed in the region. Zhangjiakou is open to such industries transferred from Beijing. The use of drones in sports, cultural and tourism industries is promoted. Beijing and Zhangjiakou will join hands in developing platforms for sports technology and cultural-creation industries, including the Zhongguancun Science Park, the Zhongguancun (Yanqing) Sports Technology Innovation Park and the New Shougang General High-end Industrial Service Park.

Enhance the sharing of public services. The development of public service facilities for sports, culture and tourism will be conducted in an integrated way. Public service facilities, such as cultural squares, museums, cultural centres, libraries, memorial halls, youth centres and youth sports clubs, will serve tourism at the same time.

The infrastructure serving all-year tourism will be improved, including airports, trains and bus stations, national and provincial road networks, gas stations along scenic routes, road-maintenance stations, sightseeing stands and tourist toilets.

In Beijing and Zhangjiakou, tourism information systems, auto campsites and services for new-energy vehicles will be improved.

Safety and emergency service systems will be upgraded. Cross-regional rescue mechanisms and outdoor sports and exploration rescue systems will be established. Systems for medical emergency assistance and pandemic control and prevention will be reinforced. All these efforts will help enhance the safety and risk surveillance, control, assessment and early-warning systems, as well as the capability of contingency response in this region.

Well-recognised Sports Events in Beijing, Tianjin and Hebei

Well-recognised outdoor fitness and recreational sports events will be held, for example:

- Marathon races in Beijing, Tianjin and Hebei;

- Mountain hiking events;

- Tour of Beijing-Tianjin-Hebei Region Tri-sport events (hiking, running, cycling);

- Tour of Beijing-Tianjin-Hebei Region cycling events;

- Beijing-Hebei Grassland Sky Road Super Marathon;

- Beijing-Zhangjiakou Great Wall International Run;

◆ Beijing-Tianjin-Hebei International Cycling Rally; and

◆ Kangbao Grassland International Marathon.

Well-recognised folk-sport events will be organised, for example:

◆ Beijing-Tianjin-Hebei kite festival;

◆ Beijing-Tianjin-Hebei martial-arts festival;

◆ Beijing-Tianjin-Hebei dragon-boat race;

◆ Beijing-Tianjin-Hebei diabolo festival;

◆ Cangzhou martial-arts festival; and

◆ Shuttlecock competitions.

Well-recognised sports events will be launched, such as Beijing-Tianjin-Hebei Province basketball, volleyball, football, badminton, table-tennis, tennis, air-volleyball, model-aircraft, triathlon (based on Tianjin triathlon) and car-racing events.

Well-recognised winter sports events will be organised, such as:

◆ Beijing-Tianjin-Hebei ice-hockey competitions;

◆ Snow-polo events;

◆ Beijing-Zhangjiakou-Chengde ice and snow carnivals;

◆ Great Mountains and Rivers, Passionate Zhangjiakou Ice and Snow Winter Fest.

Beijing-Zhangjiakou Railway Relics Park

The construction of the Beijing-Zhangjiakou Railway began in 1905 under the supervision of Zhan Tianyou, the Chinese chief engineer. It was put into operation four years later and was China' s first independently surveyed, designed, constructed and operated state-owned railway line. It represents China's modern industrial culture and spirit and is an important national cultural legacy.

It not only brought Zhangjiakou and Beijing closer in terms of time and distance, but also tells the captivating stories of generations of people, trains and social life. Over the last century, the railway has developed with the cities of Beijing and Zhangjiakou and become a part of people' s life and a witness to the cities' great changes.

Following the opening of the Beijing-Zhangjiakou High-speed Railway in 2019, the old Beijing-Zhangjiakou Railway stopped running. However, this does not mean that it has bowed out of the historical stage. The legacy of the time-honoured railway will continue to serve as Beijing-Zhangjiakou Railway Relics Park. After innovative renovation and preservation of Qinghuayuan, Qinghe, Qinglongqiao, Kangzhuang, Zhangjiakou and Xuanhua stations as well as the Zhan Tianyou Memorial Hall, it will become a modern railway relics park that combines functions of museum, sport and recreation and business.

Spartan Race

Spartan race, which debuted in 2005, is a world's top obstacle race. Over 250 races take place in 42 countries and regions across the world each year, attracting over 10 million participants. To cater to more participants, the race has also introduced group and children's races.

As an emerging sport, Spartan race is already very popular thanks to its concept of wildness, exciting competition programme and excellent competition experience. Since its introduction to China in 2016, 61 races have taken place. The locations for the race have gradually extended from the top-tier cities, such as Beijing, Shanghai, Guangzhou and Shenzhen, to across China, drawing a total of over 220,000 participants and over 1.5 billion spectators on-site and online.

In 2020, Spartan race took place for the first time in Chongli, Zhangjiakou. The three-day event drew nearly 10,000 participants. To support race participants and enthusiasts, additional high-speed trains operated between Beijing and Chongli during the race, while Chongli Ski Town provided the participants with considerate dining, accommodation and healthcare services.

Regional Tourism-Transport System for Beijing and Zhangjiakou

Aviation: In 2021, there were a total of 51 airlines operating flights from Beijing Capital International Airport, offering connections to the 175 major domestic airports. Meanwhile, a total of 13 domestic airlines operated at Beijing Daxing International Airport, offering 146 flights to 136 Chinese airports. Zhangjiakou Ningyuan Airport had 5 airlines operating 9 flights to 11 Chinese cities, including Shanghai, Hangzhou, Shenzhen and Guangzhou. Passengers may first travel to Beijing Capital International Airport or Beijing Daxing International Airport before taking subway to Beijing North Railway Station or Qinghe Railway Station, where they may travel to Zhangjiakou by the Beijing-Zhangjiakou High-speed Railway.

High-speed railway: After the opening of the Beijing-Zhangjiakou High-speed Railway, the travel from Qinghe Railway Station to Yanqing Railway Station takes only 26 minutes, and the journey from Qinghe Railway Station in Beijing to Taizicheng Railway Station in Zhangjiakou takes only 50 minutes. Tourists from Inner Mongolia and Shaanxi and Shanxi Provinces may reach Zhangjiakou by the Zhangjiakou-Hohhot High-speed Railway, Datong-Xi'an High-speed Railway or Zhangjiakou-Datong High-speed Railway. Visitors from other provinces to Zhangjiakou may first travel to Beijing by the high-speed railways from Shanghai, Guangzhou, Fuzhou and

Harbin, and then transfer to the Beijing-Zhangjiakou High-speed Railway.

Expressway: Before the Beijing-Chongli Expressway was put into operation, the journey from Beijing's 6th Ring Road to Zhangjiakou would take 3 hours and from Yanqing to Zhangjiakou 2.5 hours. Now, the travel time from Beijing's 6th Ring Road and Yanqing to Zhangjiakou have been reduced to 1.5 hours and 50 minutes respectively. Travelers from Beijing, Tianjin and Hebei may reach Zhangjiakou by taking the Capital Ring Expressway and then the Yanqing-Chongli Expressway.

Chapter 6

INTENSIFYING OLYMPIC EDUCATION AND PROMOTING SOCIAL DEVELOPMENT

The preparations for and staging of Beijing 2022 have effectively promoted the Olympic education and winter sports among 250 million primary and secondary school students across the country, which has facilitated their healthy and all-round development. A total of 835 schools have been selected as Olympic Education Demonstration Schools and 2,063 as schools with winter sports programmes.

Volunteering has become a widespread spirit across the society, thus the individuals engaged in volunteer services are increasing in China. To date, 4.436 million volunteers have registered at the Beijing Volunteer Service Federation's information platform.

Caring for and helping people with disabilities have become a public consensus. The accessible facilities have significantly increased in the host city of Beijing 2022, which has enabled the people with disabilities to integrate into social life and facilitated the building of an inclusive society.

The winter Fitness-For-All programme has been widely carried out and regular participation in physical exercise and low-carbon travel are becoming the public lifestyle. Significant social progress has been achieved, forming invaluable Games social legacies.

After Beijing 2022, to carry forward these precious legacies and the Olympic spirit, Olympic Education will be continued and volunteering will be further encouraged. Greater efforts will be made to promote the building of an inclusive society and boost the development of all social undertakings.

Intensive Development of Olympic Education

Promoted by the Games preparation, Olympic Education for the youth has seen remarkable achievements and created rich legacies with Chinese characteristics.

After the Games, Olympic Education will be intensified in schools to promote the spread of Olympic ideal and spirit in education.

• Winter sports will be popularised continuously in schools. Primary and secondary school students will be encouraged to learn winter sports skills.

• International exchanges between Chinese and foreign students will be carried out to broaden the students' international perspective and increase their knowledge about foreign cultures.

• The selection of Olympic Education Demonstration Schools, schools with winter sports programmes and "Heart to Heart Schools" will be continued and stepped up. These schools will serve as role models in carrying out Olympic Education in diverse forms and enhancing the comprehensive quality and capabilities of primary and secondary school students.

Diversified teaching for Olympic Education. Primary and secondary schools across the country will continue to incorporate Olympic Education in their curricula.

- The teaching for Olympic Education will be carried out through physical education courses and moral education programmes.

- Winter sports skills will be taught in the physical education and health classes of compulsory education.

- A system for winter sports teaching, training, competition and management in schools will be established and improved.

- The building of winter sports facilities and the training of faculty will be strengthened.

- A promotion mechanism for winter sports on campus, which involves the guidance from the government, coordination by relevant authorities and participation of various social sectors, will be in place.

- Online programmes of "Champions Talk about Beijing 2022 Spirit", "Teachers and Students Talk about Beijing 2022 Spirit", "Volunteers Talk about Beijing 2022 Spirit" and "Understand Olympic and Paralympic Winter Games" will be introduced to the primary and secondary school students on the National Smart-education Platform, sharing the stories about the Olympic Winter Games and spreading the spirit of Beijing 2022 among the students across the country.

Expand the achievements in Olympic Education. The project of selecting Olympic Education Demonstration Schools and schools with winter sports programmes will be further promoted, with a view to involving more primary and secondary schools across China to take part in Olympic Education. It is expected to have a total of 5,000 schools with winter sports programmes across China by 2025.

The building of research institutions, such as the Beijing Institute for International Olympic Studies (BIIOS), will be stepped up to produce high quality achievements in the research of winter sports and provide an international platform for Olympic Education and the training of sports professionals. On 23 June 2022, the BIIOS signed a memorandum of understanding with the International Olympic Academy in Greece. Both parties have agreed to work together in the areas of Olympic Education, teacher and student exchanges, scientific research and the promotion of Olympic culture.

Launch cultural events in Olympic Education. The popularisation of the knowledge of Olympic Winter Games and the staging of art and cultural events will continue.

• Themed education activities, such as Olympic Education lectures, Winter Olympic Education Week, education day, themed class meetings and winter camps, will continue to take place.

• Cultural activities with the elements of Olympic Winter Games, such as music, choir, dance, drama festivals and essay writing, painting, photography and knowledge contests, will be held for primary and secondary school students.

• Cultural exchange projects for Chinese and foreign youth, such as the exchange programme of "Better Future Together", and the project of "Heart to Heart Schools" will be further promoted to have more "sister schools" around the world. These international cultural-exchange events will enhance the mutual understanding and friendship between Chinese and foreign youth.

Advocating Volunteerism

Volunteer service at Beijing 2022 achieved remarkable results and played a tremendous role in the successful staging of the Games. A total of 18,000 Games volunteers and 200,000 city volunteers showed the world the upbeat image of Chinese youth with their youthful vigour and warm-hearted services despite of the difficulties and challenges, such as the COVID-19 pandemic, extreme weather and distances between competition zones.

Beijing 2022 encouraged more people to take part in volunteer services. According to statistics, China has 229 million registered volunteers and 1.32 million volunteer teams, providing nearly 5.16 billion hours of services by 18 October,

2022.

After the Games, the volunteering legacy and invaluable experience of volunteer services at Beijing 2022 will be passed down and develop. Volunteering will become a common practice across the society and promote social progress. In future, the volunteer service system will be improved and volunteer teams expanded to ensure the healthy development of volunteering in China.

Improve volunteer service systems. Systematic management of volunteer services will be encouraged and an efficient coordination mechanism involving multiple sectors and organisations will be created.

- The recruitment and registration of volunteers will be further regulated. Local residents will be accepted as volunteers according to relevant standards and requirements, and registered via different volunteer service information platforms and organisations.
- Volunteer services will be standardised and the service evaluation system improved.
- Legislation and legal service system concerning volunteering will be improved to better protect volunteers' rights and interests.
- Knowledge and skill training will be provided for volunteers to enhance their service capacity and standards.

- Incentive mechanisms for volunteering will be improved. Credits and grades will be awarded to volunteers and regulations concerning their service records and certificates will be established for the recognition of their performances and services.

Expand volunteer service platforms. Government departments and various social sectors will be involved in the building of volunteer service platforms.

- To expand the team of volunteers, incubation bases will be set up to help establish more volunteer service organisations and improve their capacity.

- Volunteer organisations that are well managed, effectively operated and widely recognised will be selected as models to give full play to their leading role in developing volunteer services.

- Volunteer service platforms will be developed to expand the areas of volunteer services and to serve more people.

- Volunteer service stations will be set up at various public service facilities wherever needed.

- Technological support will be provided to elevate the informatisation level in volunteer services. The work mode of "Internet + volunteer services" will be explored and innovations will be adopted in way of delivering service.

- Promotional platforms for volunteer services will be built to spread the spirit, culture and stories of volunteering.

- The platform and system used for the recruitment of volunteers at Beijing 2022 will be kept and improved, which will be turned into a reliable and efficient online platform for major volunteering events in Beijing.

Organise diverse volunteer service campaigns. As a resource of low-cost and high-efficiency, volunteer services are preferred in public services. Volunteer organisations will be encouraged to provide services in the undertakings of poverty alleviation, elderly and orphan care, assisting people with disabilities, disaster relief, and provision of medical and educational assistance. Volunteer teams that provide targeted and dedicated services will be formed, which will work at the grassroots level to serve the general public.

- Targeted volunteer services to help the people with financial difficulties, the elderly and people with disabilities will be encouraged.

- Based on good experience accumulated during the Beijing 2008 and Beijing 2022, volunteer services will continue to play an important role at major social events such as major conferences, exhibitions and cultural and sports events in the years to come.

- Volunteer services in emergency rescue will be further developed. Knowledge and skills related to fire safety, disaster evacuation, emergency rescue and first aid will be taught to volunteers, so that they will be able to provide better services in such work as emergency rescue, health and epidemic prevention, resettlement and psychological comforting in the event of major natural disasters and contingency actions.

- After Beijing 2022, some of the 856 Games volunteer-service points in Beijing and Zhangjiakou will be maintained to continue their services for the public.

Building an Inclusive Society

The Beijing 2022 Paralympic Winter Games have greatly raised the public's awareness of caring, assisting and respecting people with disabilities.

- Many winter sports events have been organised for people with disabilities to encourage them to engage in and enjoy winter sports.

- The significant improvement of accessibility and services in the host city have made it much easier for people with disabilities to travel and engage in social life.

- Services are also provided at the community level, including rehabilitation and care, vocational skills training and legal aid.

- A total of 666 service centres had been set up by December 2021 in Beijing, benefitting over 3.914 million people with disabilities each year. In Zhangjiakou, 75,000 and 55,000 people with disabilities received living and care subsidies respectively.

The legacies and achievements of Beijing 2022 Paralympic Winter Games will continue to serve the people with disabilities in terms of accessibility and the building of an inclusive society. Accessible environments of higher standards and better living conditions will be created to allow them to enjoy equal opportunities in their life.

Promote the application of Beijing 2022 accessibility standards. Technical standards, such as the *Accessibility Guide for the Olympic and Paralympic Winter Games Beijing 2022* and the *Atlas of Technical Standards of the Accessibility Guide for the Olympic and Paralympic Winter Games Beijing 2022*, were formulated to elevate the building standard of accessible environments in the host city and promote the revision and application of the Regulations on the Building of Accessible Environments in Beijing.

After the Games, the standards and regulations for the building of accessibility will be further improved and the assessment of the accessible facilities in new, refurbished and expanded buildings will be tightened. A regular evaluation system for accessibility will be set up to ensure the strict compliance with the laws and regulations and the proper development of accessibility in the country.

The achievements referred to in the China Accessibility

Scheme for the Olympic and Paralympic Winter Games Beijing 2022 are valuable references for the construction, management and running of the accessibility in future sports events, and will continue to promote the development of accessibility in China.

All-round development of accessibility in the country. After the Beijing 2022 Paralympic Winter Games, the accessible facilities in venues and competition zones will remain in use. Urban accessibility will be further improved, with priority given to the city roads, public transport, public service facilities, old residential areas, urban pedestrian system and smart city projects.

Technical standards for accessible Internet apps will be widely promoted. The development of accessibility to the online platforms of government administration, public services, e-business and electronic navigation will be accelerated. More user-friendly and easy-to-operate smart services will be provided to help the people with disabilities in obtaining information services. Offline instructions will be given to help them familiarise themselves with online services. Attempts will be made to build a certification system, in order to ensure that accessible facilities are standardised and regulated.

Constantly promote the building of an inclusive society. Continuous efforts will be made to create a social atmosphere of helping and supporting people with disabilities, improve their service system and enrich their spiritual and cultural life. The service quality for people with disabilities in rehabilitation, education, culture and sports will be further upgraded.

Employment for people with disabilities will be emphasised. More job opportunities will be provided to enable them to lead a happy life through their own work.

Beijing will further promote the establishment of service centres for people with disabilities in communities and townships. Services for them such as vocational rehabilitation and psychological health counselling, legal aid and volunteer services will be available for them at the grassroots level.

Promotional events will be held, including the National Day for Aiding People with Disabilities, International Day of Disabled Persons and Selection of Good News on the Causes for People with Disabilities. The knowledge and ideas related to accessibility will be promoted and people's awareness of accessible environments enhanced.

Beijing 2022 Paralympic Winter Games' Bouquets Made by People with Disabilities

The bouquets used for victory ceremonies at Beijing 2022 Paralympic Winter Games were knitted woollen flowers created using China's traditional intangible cultural heritage – Haipai weaving techniques, which had their origin in Shanghai. Over 150 people with disabilities and their family members from 10 districts in Beijing, brought together by Beijing's Centre of Hope for People with Spinal-Cord Injuries, spent over two months to create over 500 bouquets. The bouquets comprised 79,474 petals and 12,560 leaves, requiring over 6.38 million stitches and between 35 and 40 hours per bouquet. A total of over 20,000 hours were spent making them.

Chapter 7

CARRYING ON OLYMPIC CULTURAL LEGACIES

Beijing 2022 has not only delivered a sports gala, but also presented the unique Chinese culture and civilisation, perfectly integrated Chinese elements into the Olympic culture, and contributed Chinese wisdom to the sustainable development of the modern Olympic Movement.

Since the start of the Games preparation, we have created abundant winter Olympic cultural legacies including facilities, activities and products, promoted the reputation of "China-designed" and "China-made", and further disseminated the Olympic culture in China.

During these years, we united the Chinese people of all ethnic groups and conceived the great spirit of Beijing 2022, promoted cultural integration around the world, enhanced the friendship among peoples in the world, and sent out the voice of "Together for a Shared Future" .

After the Games, we will carry on the Beijing 2022 spirit, make good use of the winter Olympic cultural legacies, enhance international sports and cultural exchange, further enrich the world's Olympic culture, and embrace a brilliant future of global civilization

Carrying Forward the Beijing 2022 Spirit

A great cause generates a great spirit. In the entire lifecycle of the Games, the construction workers, staff members, volunteers and all the personnel involved worked hard together and jointly created the "Beijing 2022 Spirit", which includes "Keeping in mind the great vision, Being confident and openminded, Rising to challenges, Pursuing excellence, and Striving together for a shared future".

This represents the spiritual accomplishments of Beijing 2022, forming the most important cultural legacy and spiritual wealth of the Games.

After the Games, we will carry on the "Beijing 2022 Spirit" to inspire our people to move forward and turn it into impetus for building a modern country in all aspects.

— "Keeping in mind the great vision" means the mindset of regarding the preparation for and hosting of the Games as an initiative of national significance, striving to win honour and making contributions to the nation, actively fulfilling the missions and responsibilities, and working hard together for the benefit of the nation and the people.

— "Being confident and open-minded" means keeping a generous and inclusive mindset, displaying the sincerity and friendliness of the Chinese people through hospitality, and enhancing mutual understanding and friendship among peoples around the world.

— "Rising to challenges" means the spirit of working hard with steadfast determination, maintaining high morale to deliver on responsibilities and tackle any challenges, resolving any risks, and moving bravely forward to victory.

— "Pursuing excellence" means the spirit of being dedicated and meticulous, adhering to the highest standard and most stringent requirements in planning, design and construction, and constantly achieving breakthroughs and creating miracles.

— "Striving together for a shared future" means coordinating and working closely together, upholding the concepts of "marching towards the future together" and "enhancing solidarity", aiming for the future development of China and mankind, and calling on peoples all over the world to build a community with a shared future for mankind.

Exploring and Utilising the Cultural Legacies of Beijing 2022

Along with delivering of the Games, a rich variety of winter Olympic cultural designs, events and products were turned out to disseminate the Olympic culture and winter sports culture, through which the unique appeal of the outstanding

Chinese traditional culture, including the Great Wall, the Spring Festival and the intangible cultural heritage, were fully demonstrated, and new cultural momentum was added to the development of the Olympic Movement.

After the Games, we will further explore the Olympic cultural legacies and make good use of the Games cultural facilities to create more new cultural spaces for the residents and communities. The themed cultural and winter sports events will be continuously organised to diversify cultural services for the public. The development of the cultural creation industry with Olympic elements will be promoted constantly.

Make good use of Games cultural facilities. After the Games, we will make good use of Games cultural facilities such as the Olympic cultural squares and the Olympic Parks in the three Competition Zones, to promote the development of urban and rural public cultural service systems, expand public cultural spaces and form a high-quality, well-planned, convenient and efficient network of public cultural facilities.

Winter Olympic cultural and sports facilities will be used for public fitness, recreational and exhibition activities. Beijing 2022 cultural identifications and looks will be moved to such places as parks, public squares and museums for public exhibition, to refresh the Games memory and enrich the cultural landscape of the host city.

The building of the Beijing Olympic Museum and the Beijing Institute for International Olympic Studies will continue, which will function as unique centres for international exchange. Winter Olympic cultural and educational facilities such as the Institute for Olympic Art, Tsinghua University, Chongli Overseas Chinese Winter Sports Museum, and Zhangjiakou Taizicheng Relics will work as exchange platforms for Olympic culture, art and research.

Continuously organise winter Olympic cultural events. After the Games, public ice and snow cultural events will continue to be organised, with the scope of public engagement expanded. Specifically, the well-received public ice and snow cultural activities held at the National Public Ice and Snow Season, the National Public Ice and Snow Week and the Beijing Ice and Snow Festival will be expanded.

Olympic cultural and art events such as the International Olympic Day will be organised, and winter Olympic and winter sports knowledge learning programmes such as the "China Ice and Snow Caravan" and "Winter Sports Micro Class" will be conducted, to further popularise winter sports among the public and integrate ice and snow culture in people's daily life.

Chinese traditional ice and snow culture will be discovered, protected, exhibited and popularised, such as ice/snow sculpture, foot curling, ice game, ice dance, horse racing on snow and fur skiing, to showcase China's time-honoured traditional "ice and snow stories" and bring people new cultural experiences.

Exhibitions of winter Olympic cultural and art works, seminars, cultural and artistic creation activities, ice and snow films and TV programmes and performances of musical works will be staged, with a view to allowing winter Olympic culture and art to benefit the people and spread the Olympic Spirit and Chinese sportsmanship.

Boost Olympic cultural and artistic creation. Public cultural and artistic creation activities will be organised and creations in the forms of music, film, drama, TV programme and animation on the themes of the Olympic Games, ice and snow culture and Great Wall culture will be encouraged. The role of such resources as the China National Arts Fund, the Capital Subsidy Programme for the Creation and Production of High-quality Films and Television Works, China Art Festival, and major theatres will be put into full play in the efforts of supporting cultural and art creation.

Public cultural institutions and private sectors will be encouraged to establish in-depth cooperation in the chain of cultural licensing, creative design, production and marketing. The successful experience of Beijing 2022 in cultural and art creation will be passed on in terms of cultural resource exploration, new technology application, marketing innovation, and collaboration among enterprises, the market and universities.

Beijing and Zhangjiakou will work together to develop cultural and creative products on the themes of winter sports, the Great Wall and the Beijing-Zhangjiakou Railway, to enhance the impact of the two host cities of Beijing 2022.

Intensifying International Sports and Cultural Exchange

The preparation for Beijing 2022 sent out a strong message that China and other countries are united and marching "together for a shared future". China has maintained close and positive relations with the IOC and international sports organisations, ensured that the preparatory work for the Games met the Olympic standards, provided good services to the NOCs and NPCs, offered warm hospitality to athletes and guests from different countries, had 173 countries jointly sign the Olympic Truce, and expanded cultural and economic exchange through sports, thus making Beijing 2022 into a real catalyst for China's opening up to the world.

After the Games, Beijing 2022 will continue its role in enhancing the cultural exchange between China and other nations and the dialogue among civilisations, deepening the cooperation with all international sports organisations, further broadening the communication with the countries advanced in winter sports, sister cities and Olympic cities, promoting non-governmental cultural cooperation and exchange, and bringing international sports exchange to a new level.

Deepen the cooperation with international sports organisations. After the Games,

- The cooperation with the IOC, the IPC and IFs will be further enhanced to introduce to China more top-level international sports events.
- The communication with sister cities and NOCs will continue to be consolidated to organise cultural and sports exchange activities together, including training programmes, friendship competitions and cultural visits.
- New approaches for sports exchange with countries advanced in winter sports and Olympic cities will be explored to broaden and deepen the exchange and cooperation in winter sports, ice and snow industry and culture, thus further promoting the sustainable development of winter sports in China.

Relying on its influence as the host city for both summer and winter editions of the Olympic Games, Beijing will actively invite international sports organisations, international winter sports institutions, and well-known international ice and snow enterprises to Beijing to popularise winter sports and expand China's winter sports market, and contribute to the development of Beijing as an international communication centre.

Broaden international cooperation in multiple fields. The experience in international exchange gained during Beijing 2022 will be applied in enhancing the international influence of well-known cultural events such as the "Happy Spring Festival" and "Meet in Beijing" International Arts Festivals.

The Chinese cultural industry will use the rich and diverse historical and cultural resources of the country to develop cultural and tourism products that cater for the interest of overseas customers. The domestic cities will be encouraged to join hands in developing international cooperation in the cultural and tourism industries.

Various international organisations will be invited to have their annual meetings, exhibitions and conventions staged in China, with a view to promoting the cooperation in such fields as economy, culture, tourism and education. Digital technology will be used in promoting online international exchange activities such as "cloud exchange and communication" .

Conduct various forms of non-governmental exchange. Enterprises and institutions, non-governmental organisations and private organs will be encouraged to use their own advantages to organise international cultural and sports exchange activities.

- China's overseas institutions, including Chinese language schools, overseas Chinese organisations and communities, industrial and commerce associations, townsmen association, as well as art and cultural societies, will be encouraged to play their role in cultural exchange and communication;

- A few neighbourhood communities will also be engaged in promoting grassroots international exchange;

- Chinese folk ice and snow sports will be introduced to the world; and

- International exchanges with Olympic cities through such platforms as the World Union of Olympic Cities will be expanded, further advancing the non-governmental international exchange in Olympic sports and culture.

Over One Thousand Winter Olympic Pins Exhibited at Beijing Olympic Forest Park

During Beijing 2022, an Olympic pin exhibition under the theme of "Charm of Olympic City - The Stories of Beijing on Olympic Pins" was held at the Beijing 2022 Main Media Centre (MMC), to showcase Beijing's urban culture to reporters from around the world. After the Games, nearly 1,000 pins were moved to the "Olympics Exhibition Hall" at the Beijing Olympic Forest Park for long-term exhibition, which is open to the public free of charge. "Small Pins, Great Culture" , these pins have recorded the changes and transformation of Beijing as a host city for both summer and winter editions of the Olympic Games, giving visitors the opportunity to appreciate the Olympic Spirit and the culture of Beijing.

"A Thousand Screens in a Hundred Cities" UHD TV Promotion Campaign

Immediately after the UHD TV Promotion Campaign was launched, many regions across the country made active response and led the way in the campaign. A lot of big UHD outdoor screens and 8K TVs were installed in those regions before Beijing 2022, to ensure the successful UHD live-streaming of the Games. Through 8K live-streaming practice during Beijing 2022, the UHD TV Promotion Campaign has become a novelty widely recognised by the people.

Today, the UHD TV Promotion Campaign has officially entered the operational stage. It will effectively meet the demand of citizens across the country for watching UHD TV programmes and experiencing novel visual/audio technology, and expand the new visual/audio public service for citizens.

Beijing Olympic City Development Association

Beijing Olympic City Development Association (BODA) is the legacy organisation for both Beijing 2008 and Beijing 2022. Committed to its mission of "carrying on the Olympic spirit and building a better city" and its work philosophy of "seeking innovative, harmonious and win-win development", BODA plays an active role in promoting the sustainable development of the Olympic Movement, implementing the national strategy of fitness for all, and quickening the pace of building a leading sports nation and a Healthy China.

According to its strategic objectives, BODA will strengthen the top-level design, innovate its working systems and mechanisms, constantly improve its capability of carrying on Olympic legacies, and promote high-quality development of the city.

To this end, BODA will

- Give full play to its role as an institution for carrying on Olympic legacies; properly manage and utilise the Olympic legacies; organise events including the Beijing Olympic City Sports and Cultural Festival, Beijing International Sports Film Festival, Olympic Education Programme, and cultural promotional activities; speed up the construction of the Beijing Olympic Museum; publicise the Olympic Movement and the city of Beijing; and continuously consolidate its role in spreading the Olympic spirit and carrying on

Olympic legacies.

- Give full play to its role in international exchange; intensify communication, cooperation and mutual learning with international organisations including the IOC, IFs, SportAccord, UMVO, Olympic Museums Network, and International Sport Movies TV Federation; and build itself into a "special window" to display the construction of Beijing into an international exchange centre.

- Give full play to its role in promoting sharing and mutual learning; build an effective platform to coordinate the sharing of Olympic legacies; summarise the practical experience and Olympic knowledge of Beijing; continuously conduct Olympic legacy research and application to lay a foundation for sustainably carrying on Olympic legacies; and build a high-end think tank to share the experience in hosting major sports and other events.

- Give full play to its driving role in carrying on the Olympic legacies; coordinate the tangible and intangible Olympic legacies, and sports, cultural and tourism resources; strengthen cooperation among different cities and regions; actively offer suggestions on the post-Games utilisation of Olympic venues; work together with Yanqing District and Zhangjiakou City to build a network of museums; enhance the cooperation in Olympic legacy programmes; and contribute to the construction of the Beijing-Zhangjiakou Sports, Cultural and Tourism Belt.

一起向未来

Together for a Shared Future